Progressive
RHYTHM
Guitar

by
Gary Turner and Brenton White

Visit our Website
www.learntoplaymusic.com

The Progressive Series of Music Instruction Books, CDs, and DVDs

2

Acknowledgments
Photographs: Phil Martin

For further information contact:
LTP Publications
Email: info@learntoplaymusic.com.au
www.learntoplaymusic.com

I.S.B.N. 0 959540 47 4
Order Codes: CP-54047

CONTENTS

Introduction 5
Tuning Your Guitar 5
Solid Body Electric, Steel String Acoustic 6
Seating, The Pick 7

SECTION 1
Lesson 1   Chord diagrams, A and D chords, right hand position, the left hand 9
2   Musical terms, rhythm patterns, chord progression, pivot finger 11
3   E chord, 12 bar blues, new rhythm patterns, rhythm variations 13
4   G and C chords, first string notes, the quarter note, tablature 16
5   Turnaround No. 1, second string notes, ...18
6   F chord, Turnaround No. 2, third string notes, the half note 19
7   A7, D7, and E7 chords, fourth string notes 21
8   Continuous right hand movement, fifth string notes, the eighth note . . .23
9   Alternative chord fingerings,
       G7 and C7 chords, alternative chord forms, two bar rhythms 25
10 Blues in E, sixth string notes,
       the whole note, the dotted half note, the dotted quarter note 27
11 Note Summary, note values, bass note picking 29
12 Time signature, ¾ time, bass note picking (¾ time) 31
13 Am and Dm chords, bass note runs 32
14 Cmaj7 and Fmaj7 chords, sixteenth note rhythm patterns 33
15 Amaj7, Dmaj7 and Gmaj7 chords, maj7 progression, chromatic scale 35
16 Chromatic note summary,
       progression in A, experiments in bass note picking 37
17 Bm chord, triplet rhythm, Turnaround 1 in D 39
18 E6 and A6 chords, Blues in E, the major scale 41
19 "Rock" chords, 12 bar in A, Rock chord variation 43
20 Asus, Dsus and Esus chords, G major scale 46
21 The hammer on, the pull off 48
Section One Summary, extra progressions 50

SECTION 2
Lesson 22 The Bar chord, root 6 bar chord, root 6 bar chord progression 54
23 Progression in F, the percussive strum (bar and open chords) 56
24 Bar chord progression, key signatures 58
25 Root 6 minor bar chord, minor bar chord progressions 59
26 Two bar percussive rhythm, summary of scales and key signatures 60
27 Dominant 7th bar chord (root 6), Blues in F, rests in music 62
28 Right hand deadening technique, eighth note rests 64
29 Staccato strumming 66
30 Root 5 bar chord, 12 bar in G 67
31 Basic blues patterns, 1&2 69
32 Dampening technique 71

4

CONTENTS CONTINUED

Lesson 33 "Rock" chords, Blues pattern No. 3 72

            34 Root 5 minor bar chord, root 5 minor bar chord progression 74

            35 Turnaround patterns 75

            36 Right hand rhythm techniques 77

            37 Left & right hand rhythm techniques, chord construction-major chords 78

            38 Dominant 7th bar chord (root 5), reggae rhythms 80

            39 Arpeggio picking, arpeggio variations 82

            40 Arpeggio picking with bass note runs, chord construction-minor chords . . .84

            41 Min7th chords, chord construction-dom7th and min7th chords 85

            42 Major 6th chords, 7th chords - "rock" form .87

            43 Rock rhythm 89

            44 Simple and compound time, $\frac{6}{8}$ time examples 90

            Section Two Summary, extra progressions 92

SECTION 3

            45 Bar chord formations 96

            46 Suspended chords, suspended example 98

            47 Major seventh chords 99

            48 Off beat rhythms 101

            49 Ninth chords, chord substitution, turnaround in A, Jazz Blues in B♭ . . .102

            50 Augmented chords, augmented example 104

            51 Diminished chords 106

            52 Root 6 6th chord-alternative form, root 6 m7th chords-alternative form,
                  root 6 m6th chords, Jazz Blues in G 107

            53 Dominant 7th chord-alternative form, 12 bar in D 110

            54 New sixteenth note rhythm, sixteenth note variations 112

            Section Three Summary, extra progressions 114

Appendix One: Tuning, tuning hints 119

Appendix Two: Song list, sheet music 120

Appendix Three: Transposing, capo 122

Appendix Four: Groups 125

Appendix Five: Minor keys 126

Chord formula chart, altered chords, scale tone chords 128

Glossary of musical terms 131

INTRODUCTION

Progressive Rhythm Guitar will provide you with an essential guide into the styles and technique of rhythm guitar playing. As a rhythm guitarist you will be required to: -

(a) Play chords to accompany a vocal or instrumental melody line, and
(b) Help establish the beat of a particular song. (e.g. rock, reggae, waltz etc.)

Within the three main sections of this book a lesson by lesson structure has been used to give a clear and carefully graded method of study. No prior knowledge on your behalf is assumed.

Aside from the specific aim of teaching rhythm guitar, basic music theory has been introduced to help you to understand the material being presented. Theory can often be applied to solve practical problems and hence aid in your future development.

From the beginning you should set yourself a goal. Many people learn guitar because of a desire to play like their favourite artist or to play a certain style of music (e.g. rock, funk, reggae etc.). Motivations such as these will help you to persevere through the more difficult sections of work. As you develop it will be important to adjust and update your goals.

It is important to have a correct approach to practice. You will benefit more from several short practices (e.g. 15-30 minutes per day) than one or two long sessions per week. This is especially so in the early stages, because of the basic nature of the material being studied. In a practice session you should divide your time evenly between the study of new material and the revision of past work. It is a common mistake for semi-advanced students to practice only the pieces they can already play well. Although this is more enjoyable, it is not a very satisfactory method of practice. You should also try to correct mistakes and experiment with new ideas.

It is the author's belief that an experienced teacher will be an invaluable aid to your progress.

TUNING YOUR GUITAR

Before you commence each lesson or practice session you will need to tune your guitar. If your guitar is out of tune everything you play will sound incorrect even though you are holding the correct notes. The first track on the CD contains the notes of the six open strings of the guitar. 1.0 is the open 6th string (low E note), 1.1 is the open A string, 1.2 is the open D string, etc.

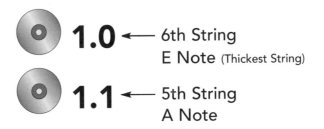

1.0 ← 6th String
E Note (Thickest String)

1.1 ← 5th String
A Note

SOLID BODY ELECTRIC

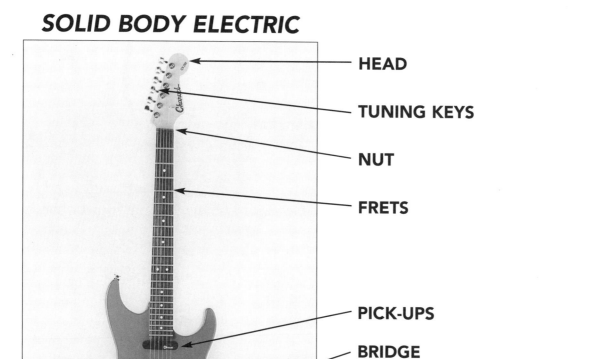

- HEAD
- TUNING KEYS
- NUT
- FRETS
- PICK-UPS
- BRIDGE
- PICK-UP SWITCH
- VOLUME & TONE CONTROLS

STEEL STRING ACOUSTIC

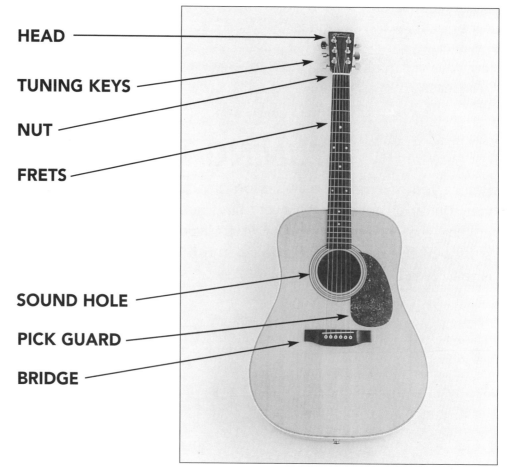

- HEAD
- TUNING KEYS
- NUT
- FRETS
- SOUND HOLE
- PICK GUARD
- BRIDGE

SEATING

Before you commence playing, a comfortable seating position is required. Most modern guitarists prefer to sit with their right leg raised, as shown in the photograph. The guitar should be held close to the body, and in a vertical position. The main aim is for comfort and easy access to the guitar.

THE PICK

The contact between the right hand and the strings is made with the use of a pick (also called a plectrum), which is held between the thumb and index finger:

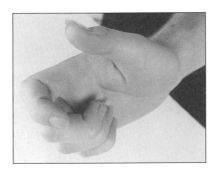

1. Index finger curved.

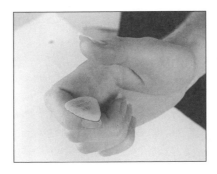

2. Pick placed on index finger with its point about 1/4 inch (1cm) past the finger-tip.

3. Thumb clamps down, holding the pick in place.

Picks are usually made of plastic, and come in a variety of different shapes and thickness. (Try a .46 mm light gauge Jim Dunlop.)

SECTION ONE

LESSON ONE

CHORD DIAGRAMS

Chords are written on a **chord diagram**. This chord diagram shows you exactly where to place your left hand fingers in order to play a particular chord. A chord diagram is a grid of horizontal and vertical lines representing the strings and frets of the guitar. The chord diagram below illustrates an **open E major** chord.

LEFT HAND FINGERING

1 Index Finger
2 Middle Finger
3 Ring Finger
4 Little Finger

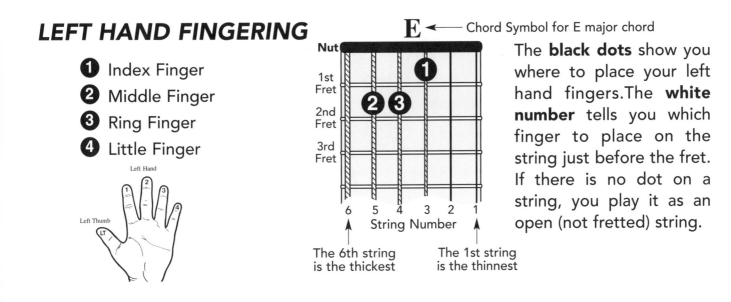

Chord Symbol for E major chord

The **black dots** show you where to place your left hand fingers. The **white number** tells you which finger to place on the string just before the fret. If there is no dot on a string, you play it as an open (not fretted) string.

The 6th string is the thickest

The 1st string is the thinnest

CHORDS: A MAJOR, D MAJOR

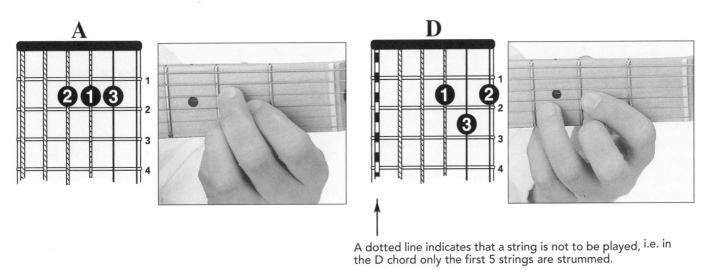

A dotted line indicates that a string is not to be played, i.e. in the D chord only the first 5 strings are strummed.

Position each chord carefully, placing the first finger down, then the second, finally the third. Each finger must be placed directly behind the fret, and on its tip (this usually means that the last finger joint is bent). Check with the photographs to ensure that the correct fingering is being used.

* This is a shorthand method of writing A major. It applies to all major chords.

RIGHT ARM POSITION

The correct position for the right arm is illustrated in **Photo A** below. Notice that the forearm rests on the upper edge of the guitar, just below the elbow. Be careful not to have the elbow hanging over the face of the guitar or your hand too far along the fretboard (**Photo B**).

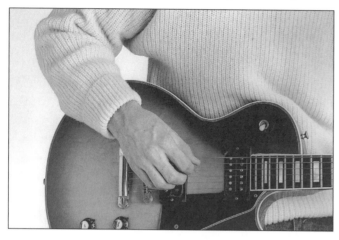

Photo A: CORRECT

Photo B: INCORRECT

THE LEFT HAND

The left hand fingers are numbered as such:

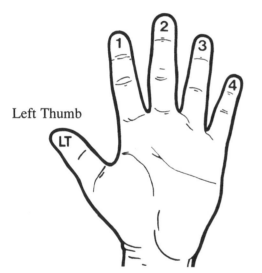

Left Thumb

LEFT HAND PLACEMENT

Your fingers should be **on their tips** and placed just **behind** the frets (not on top of them).

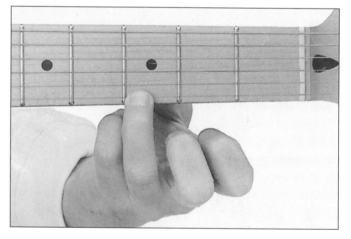

Be careful not to allow the thumb to hang too far over the top of the neck (**Photo C**), or to let it run parallel along the back of the neck (**Photo D**).

Photo C: INCORRECT

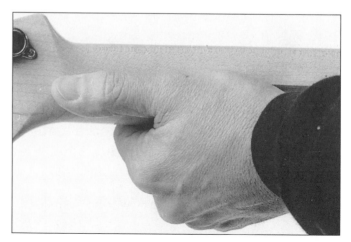

Photo D: INCORRECT

LESSON TWO

MUSICAL TERMS

Songs can be written in the form of a chord progression, which makes use of various musical terms that you will need to know:

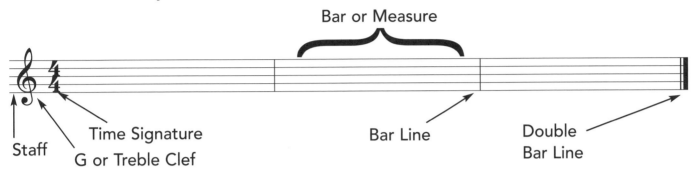

Staff - consists of 5 parallel lines, between which there are 4 spaces.

Treble Clef - (sometimes called 'G' clef) a sign placed at the beginning of each staff of music.

Time Signature - consists of two numbers; the top one indicating the number of beats per bar, and the bottom one indicating the type of beat. (Its use will become clearer to you as chord progressions are introduced. For now, you can think of the time signature as being the deciding factor in whether a song has a rock, waltz of march beat.)

Bar Line - a vertical line drawn across the staff which divides the music into sections called bars or measures.

Double Bar Line - marks either the end of the progression, or the end of an important section of it.

RHYTHM PATTERNS

V This is a wedge mark, which indicates one down strum. The adjacent rhythm pattern shows 4 down strums per bar. To help keep the beat, tap your foot as you count and strum. Remember to count in groups of 4.

TROUBLE-SHOOTING

Do the chords sound clear? Try strumming them again, but this time very slowly so that the pick glides across each string individually. If you hear buzzing or deadening sounds on any string, check the following points:

1. Fingers on their tips (compare with photographs).
2. Fingers directly behind frets - not on the fret, or too far behind it.
3. Pressure applied firmly and continuously (do not release the pressure on the strings until you are about to change chords).
4. Thumb NOT hanging too far over the top of the neck.
5. Guitar in tune (see Appendix One).

CHORD PROGRESSION

Using the given rhythm pattern, play the following chord progression:

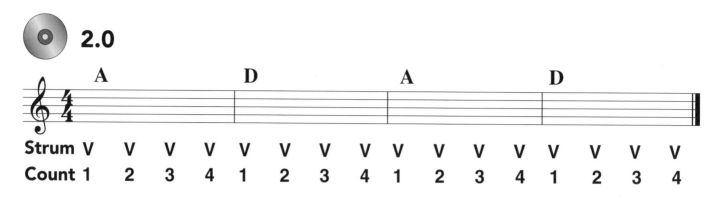

PIVOT FINGER

When changing from A to D, the first finger remains in position on the 2nd fret of the 3rd string, and acts as a pivot around which the other fingers move. This is an important technique, making many chord changes easier and smoother.

Timing is of the utmost importance, so keep a slow, steady count. Smooth chord changes are far more desirable than speed at this stage of your development. Speed will come with time and practice (be patient).

TROUBLE-SHOOTING

1. Memorize each chord as it is introduced. Be careful to use the correct fingering.
2. Play slowly at first, concentrating on chord changes.
3. Tap your foot with the beat and count 1....2....3....4 aloud.

LESSON THREE

E CHORD

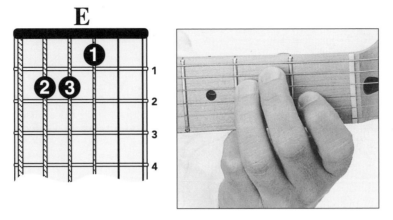

Instead of changing the strumming for each bar it is quite common to play the same pattern of strums throughout the chord progression. This is called a **rhythm pattern**. It is placed above the staff and represents which strumming pattern is played in each bar of music.

The following progression uses the 3 chords studied so far: A, D and E.

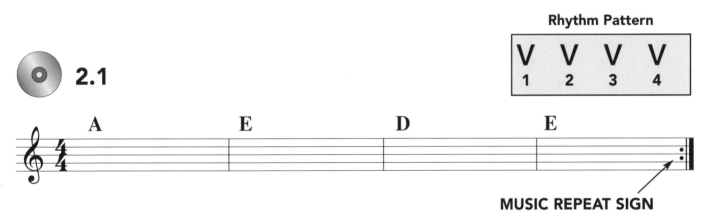

Music Repeat Sign - This indicates that the progression is repeated from the beginning. After the repeat, finish on a single strum of the opening chord (in this case, an A chord). This practice will apply to most progressions in this book.

Slide Finger - When changing from an A major chord to an E major chord the first finger slides to the new position without being lifted off the third string. The same sliding technique is used between the D and E chord changes.

12 BAR BLUES

12 Bar Blues is a pattern of chords which repeats every 12 bars. This progression is invaluable to the rock guitarist because of its use in many songs. For example, songs performed by Elvis Presley, Chuck Berry and the Beatles, such as "Hound Dog", "Johnny B. Goode" and "Roll over Beethoven" are all based upon a 12 bar progression (see Appendix Two).

2.2

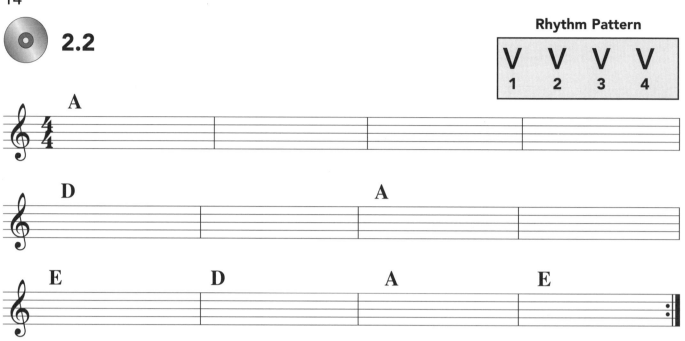

Rhythm Pattern

V	V	V	V
1	2	3	4

You will notice that in the first line there is no chord symbol written over the 2nd, 3rd and 4th bars. It is unnecessary to repeat a chord symbol until an actual chord change occurs (e.g. at the 5th bar). This rule applies to all chord progressions studied in this book.

NEW RHYTHM PATTERNS

You are already familiar with the down strum symbol which was introduced in the last lesson. To make rhythm patterns more interesting, a combination of down and up strums can be used. An up strum is indicated by an inverted wedge mark, ∧ , and will follow a down strum. Try the following rhythm using an A major chord. End each rhythm pattern with a single strum.

3.0

On the 'number' count a down strum is played, and on the 'and' count (indicated +) an up strum is played. The down strum corresponds with the foot tap ('on' the beat) and the up strum corresponds with the raising of the foot ('off' the beat.) Thus there are two strums for every beat. Here is a variation on the above rhythm, using the down/up strum on the 2nd beat only.

3.1

Memorize and practice this rhythm, holding the A chord. Once this is done, you can apply it to the chord progression in Example 2. Watch your timing.

* This is a repeat sign indicating an exact repeat of the previous bar.

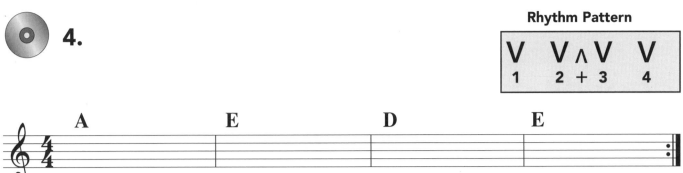

4.

Rhythm Pattern

V	V ∧ V	V
1	2 + 3	4

A   E   D   E

RHYTHM VARIATIONS

Here are some of the variations using down/up strums. You will be able to apply these rhythms to most chord progressions in $\frac{4}{4}$ time. Play each rhythm pattern four times and end each by a single strum of the A major chord.

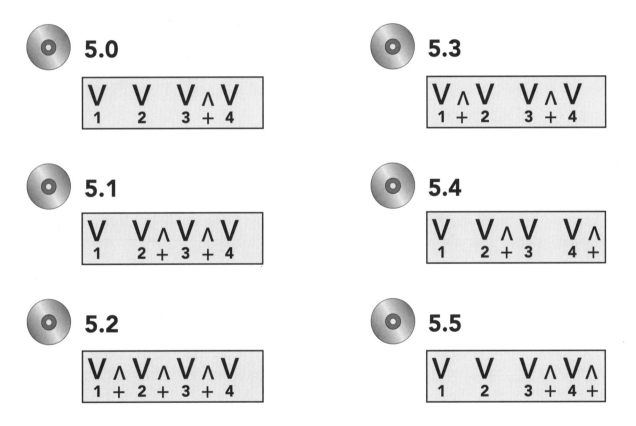

5.0

V	V	V ∧ V
1	2	3 + 4

5.1

V	V ∧ V ∧ V
1	2 + 3 + 4

5.2

V ∧ V ∧ V ∧ V
1 + 2 + 3 + 4

5.3

V ∧ V	V ∧ V
1 + 2	3 + 4

5.4

V	V ∧ V	V ∧
1	2 + 3	4 +

5.5

V	V	V ∧ V ∧
1	2	3 + 4 +

Experiment with any other combinations that you can think of. Try one new rhythm pattern each day.

TROUBLE-SHOOTING

Does your rhythm strumming sound even and pleasant to the ear?
Check the following points:

1. Guitar in tune.
2. Strum lightly and smoothly, with a combination of arm and wrist movement. A lightly held pick will encourage light strumming.
3. Keep wrist relaxed, to gain maximum movement.

LESSON FOUR

CHORDS G AND C

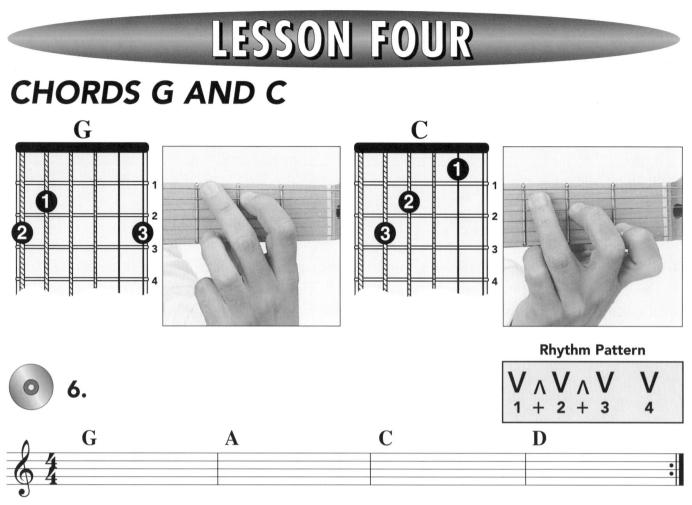

Rhythm Pattern

V ∧ V ∧ V V
1 + 2 + 3 4

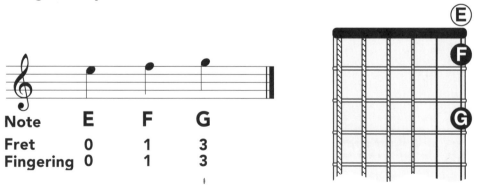

6.

You can also use any of the 4/4 rhythm patterns introduced in Lesson Three. Remember to finish the progression on a single strum of the opening chord (G). Use the pivot finger principle for the chord change A to C (i.e. 2nd finger pivot).

NOTES ON THE FIRST STRING

A basic knowledge of notes and their position on the staff is important to help you understand the theory discussed throughout this book. Notes in the first position (i.e. the first 4 frets) will gradually be introduced over the next 7 lessons.

Note	E	F	G
Fret	0	1	3
Fingering	0	1	3

General rule: For first position playing, the first number and fret number will be the same; e.g. notes on the first fret are played with the first finger. 'O' indicates an open string.

* It is not the aim of this book to cover note work in a comprehensive manner, since rhythm guitar predominantly involves chord work. Notes are covered fully in Progressive Guitar Method.

THE QUARTER NOTE

This is a quarter note, or crotchet, worth one count. Notes should be played with a downward motion of the pick. The quarter note has the same timing as one down strum; both are worth one count. Once again, remember to keep the count even.

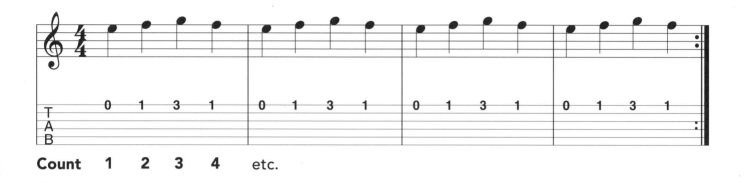

Count   **1**   **2**   **3**   **4**   etc.

Try some other combinations of first string notes, saying the names of each note aloud as you play them. This will help you learn the note names, as well as their positions on the guitar. Note exercises will also help to 'loosen up' your fingers.

TABLATURE

Under the music notes you will notice a method of notating music called tablature (TAB). Tablature is a method of indicating the position of notes on the fretboard. There are six 'tab' lines, each representing one of the six strings on the guitar:

* Note readers may need to refer to the tablature to determine the position of an example.

When a number is placed on one of the lines, it indicates the fret location of a note, e.g.

This indicates the 3rd fret of the first string (a G note)

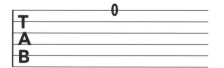

This indicates the first string open (an E note).

You can read the time values by following the count written beneath the tab.

LESSON FIVE

TURNAROUND PROGRESSION NO.1

The turnaround is another very important progression for you to become familiar with because, like 12 bar blues, it is the basis for many songs (see Appendix Two). In this turnaround, a new chord, E minor, is introduced (the abbreviation 'm' is used to indicate a minor chord).

Try the next example using the suggested rhythm pattern and then apply any of the other rhythm patterns introduced in Lesson Three. Remember to repeat the progression, and then finish with a single strum of the first chord (G).

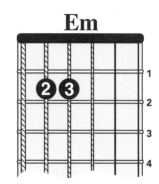

7.

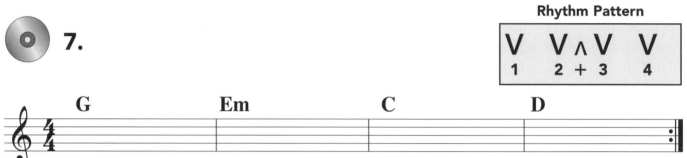

NOTES ON THE SECOND STRING

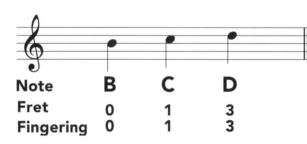

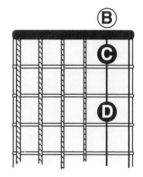

Try a combination of the first and second string notes:

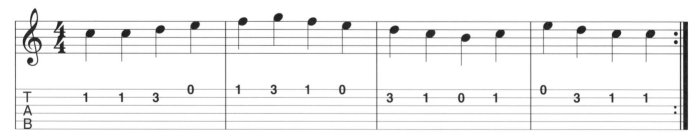

TROUBLE-SHOOTING

Note playing can present you with new problems not previously encountered in chord work. The following points should be observed:

1. Fingers on tips and directly behind frets.
2. Hold strings firmly against fretboard.
3. Use correct fingering (first finger - first fret, second finger - second fret, etc.).
4. Left hand fingers must remain close to the strings at all times; e.g. when an open string is played, your fingers should still be in close proximity.

LESSON SIX

F CHORD

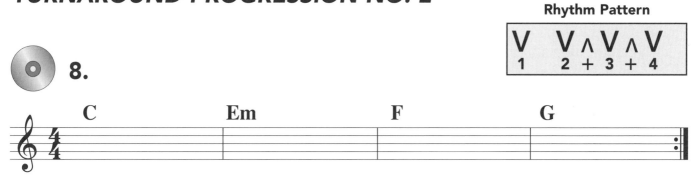

In the F chord the first finger bars across two strings, tilting slightly to the left. This is a difficult chord to play, and will need much practice. Try combining it with the chords already studied; making up your own examples, or trying simple songs.

TURNAROUND PROGRESSION NO. 2

Rhythm Pattern

V		V	∧	V	∧	V
1		2	+	3	+	4

8.

| C | Em | F | G |

This turnaround is in the key of C major. The key of a song is generally indicated by the opening chord, e.g. Turnaround No. 1 (Lesson Five) is in the key of G major.

NOTES ON THE THIRD STRING

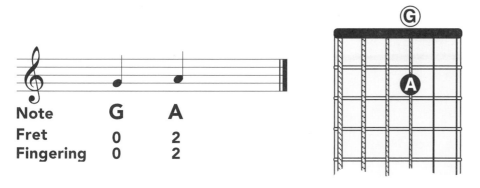

Note	G	A
Fret	0	2
Fingering	0	2

You now have two G notes; one on the first string and one on the third string. This repetition occurs with all notes, since the musical alphabet only contains seven letter names (A to G). The two G's that you now know are said to be one octave apart.

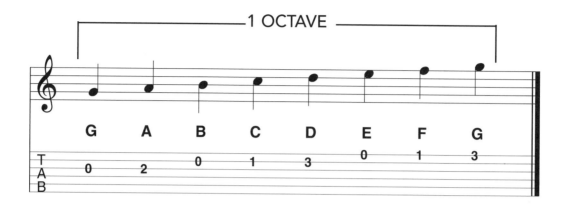

THE HALF NOTE

This is a half note, or minim, worth two counts. Two half notes make up a complete bar in $\frac{4}{4}$ time, and in the example below (bar 2) notes are played on the first and third counts.

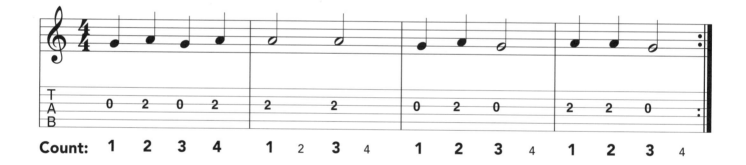

Hold the half note for its full value of two counts. Tap your foot with the beat.

LESSON SEVEN

*CHORDS A7, D7 and E7**

There are three main types of chords, namely, majors, minors and sevenths. So far you have had examples of majors and minors; three seventh chords are introduced below: -

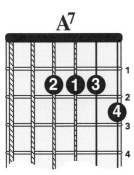

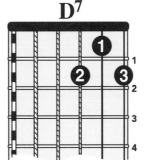

An optional fingering for the above A7 chord is shown below. The first finger bars 3 strings.

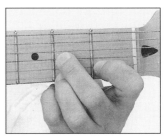

The use of the seventh chords as substitutions for major chords can make the 12 bar blues progression more interesting:

9.0

Rhythm Pattern

V	∧	V	V
1	+	2	3	4

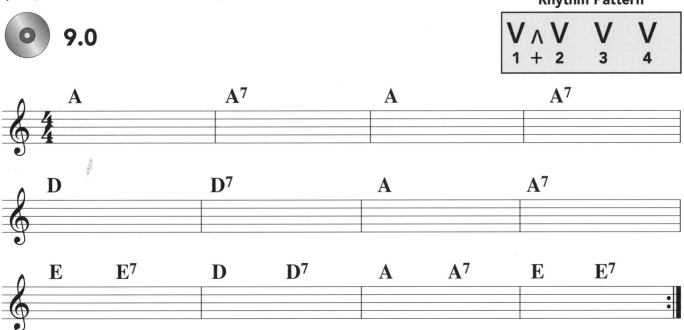

You will notice in bars 9 to 12, that there are two chords per bar. Each chord is given two counts. Once the suggested rhythm pattern has been mastered, try some other variations (more difficult) of down and down/up strumming.

* The correct name for these chords is 'Dominant Seventh,' however the name is often abbreviated to 'Seventh' and written as such.

In any turnaround a seventh chord may be played in the last bar, in place of the major chord; e.g. Turnaround No.1 in the key of G: -

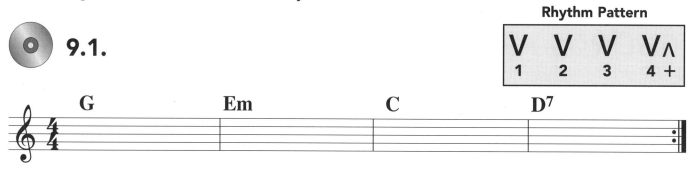

This seventh chord (D7) will 'resolve' (i.e. lead back) to the first chord (in this case, G).

NOTES ON THE FOURTH STRING

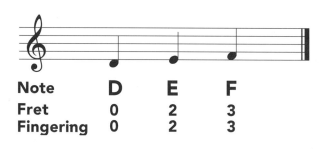

Note	D	E	F
Fret	0	2	3
Fingering	0	2	3

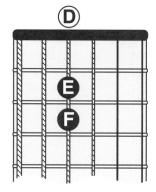

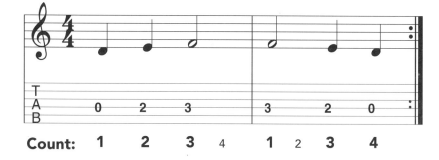

Count: 1   2   3   4   1   2   3   4

LESSON EIGHT

CONTINUOUS RIGHT HAND MOVEMENT

All of the rhythm patterns that you have so far studied involve continuous right hand movement. This right hand movement can be represented thus:

If you consider the most basic rhythm | v v v v| the right hand is actually playing four down strums across the strings (producing the sound) and also playing four up strums away from the strings. The up strums, which produce no sound, are represented by broken wedge marks ⋀. Hence the basic rhythm can be represented thus:

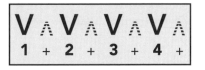

Illustrating continuous right hand movement. This principle is important in the following rhythm, where a down strum is played away from the guitar on the third beat (indicated by the broken wedge mark):

Say aloud: down up down up ..... up down up

This rhythm is extremely important, and should be applied to all progressions so far studied. You should not proceed until it is mastered.

9.2

Rhythm Pattern

G   Em   C   D⁷

NOTES ON THE FIFTH STRING

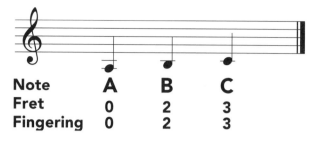 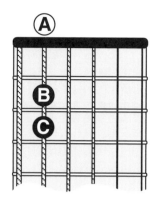

Note	A	B	C
Fret	0	2	3
Fingering	0	2	3

The notes on the fifth string use leger lines, which are small horizontal lines upon which notes are written when their pitch is above or below the staff.

THE EIGHTH NOTE

This is an eighth note, or quaver, worth half a count. Two eighth notes, which are sometimes joined by a bar, ♪♪ have the same value as a quarter note (1 beat). Eighth notes are counted:

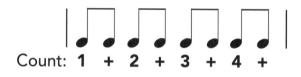

Count: **1 + 2 + 3 + 4 +**

which can be compared to the timing of a bar of down/up strums:

V ∧ V ∧ V ∧ V ∧
1 + 2 + 3 + 4 +

10.

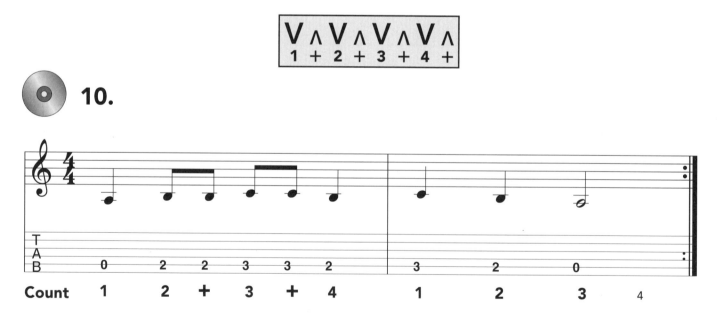

LESSON NINE

ALTERNATING CHORD FINGERINGS

In many situations the standard fingering for a chord can be altered to make a specific chord progression easier to play. Consider Turnaround No.1 in the key of G:

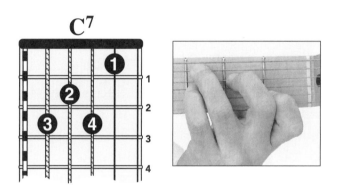

If the Em chord is played with the first and second fingers (instead of the second and third), then the pivot finger principle can be applied as such:
G to Em: First finger acts as a pivot, remaining on the fifth string at the second fret.
Em to C: Second finger acts as a pivot, remaining on the fourth string at the second fret. This will make these chord changes easier and smoother.
You must select alternative chord fingerings carefully. In most cases the conventional fingering will be best; any other fingerings used will be determined by either the preceding or following chords.

CHORDS G7 AND C7

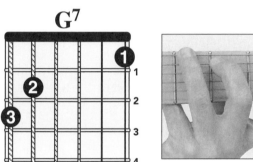

When playing the G7 chord make sure that the first string sounds clear.

The C7 chord can be formed from a C chord by adding the fourth finger.

ALTERNATIVE CHORD FORMS

There are many different ways of playing the same chord, for example, in many progressions the following shapes for A7 and E7 may be more suitable:

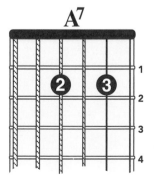

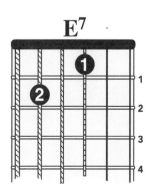
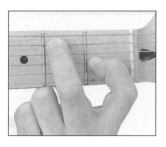

Try the following progressions, using the two alternative shapes introduced on the previous page, and the new chords G7 and C7.

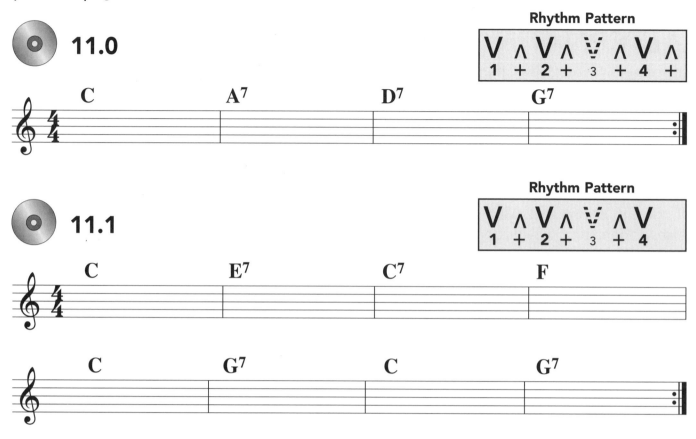

TWO BAR RHYTHMS

In all of the rhythms studied so far, the pattern is repeated for every bar. Thus these patterns are referred to as 'one bar rhythms.' However, during the course of a song or chord progression, the rhythm pattern may change. For example, a two bar rhythm pattern may be used throughout: -

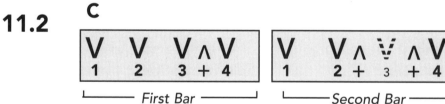

Applied to the chord progression in Example 11.0 this two bar rhythm can be represented as such:

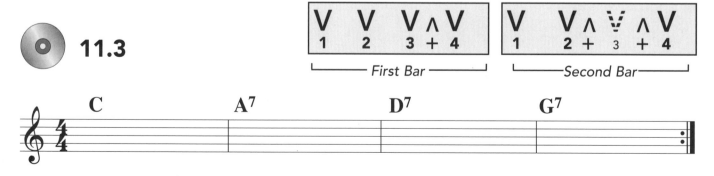

Experiment with other two bar rhythm combinations.

LESSON TEN

BLUES IN E

Blues in E introduces a new chord, B7. Some guitarists deaden the 6th string by lightly touching it with the left hand thumb which reaches over the top of the neck (see photo). The 6th string can then be strummed but it won't sound as it is deadened. This technique can apply to any chord where the 6th string note is not a part of that chord shape.

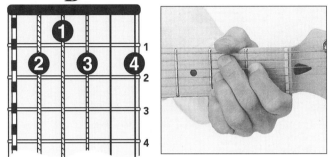

B⁷

Rhythm Pattern

12.

This blues introduces 'first and second endings'. On the first time through, ending one is played (1. ⎤), then the progression is repeated (as indicated by the repeat sign,) and ending two is played (2. ⎤). Be careful not to play both endings together.

When changing from E7 to B7 (and vice versa) the second finger acts as a pivot (see Lesson 2). You should be constantly looking for 'short cuts' in chord changes, such as this pivot finger principle.

NOTES ON THE SIXTH STRING

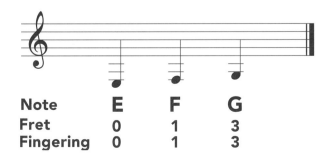

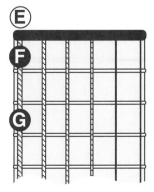

Note	E	F	G
Fret	0	1	3
Fingering	0	1	3

THE WHOLE NOTE

This is an whole note, or semibreve, worth 4 counts. In 4/4 time it is held for a full bar.

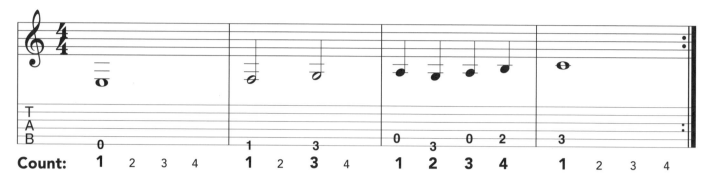

THE DOTTED HALF NOTE

A dot, placed after a note, increases the value of that note by a half; e.g. a dotted half note will be worth 3 counts:

has the same value as

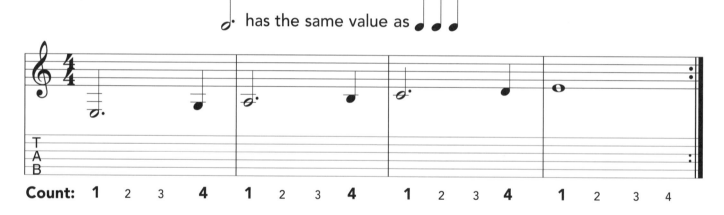

THE DOTTED QUARTER NOTE

A dotted quarter note will be worth 1 and 1/2 counts.

has the same value as

Thus the dot itself does not have a specific value, it depends upon which note it follows.

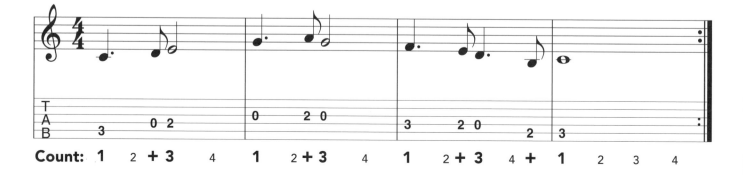

LESSON ELEVEN

NOTE SUMMARY: OPEN POSITION

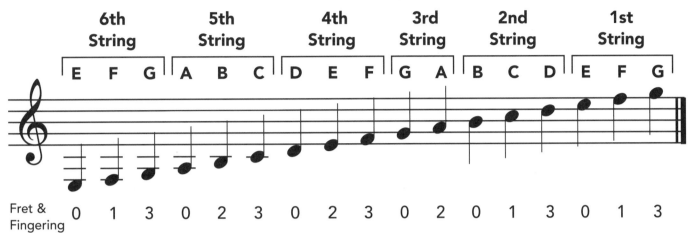

The open position on the guitar includes all the notes so far studied (as written above). You will need to be familiar with all of them, as they will be used in future examples. Starting from the bass note E, play up to the top G and back down again, naming each note aloud as you play it. Keep a slow, steady beat.

By playing through the notes you will notice that B to C and E to F are only one fret apart (called a semitone), whereas all other notes are two frets apart (called a tone). The distance between notes of the musical alphabet can be set out as such:

semitone (i.e. one fret apart)

It is essential for you to remember this pattern of notes.

NOTE AND REST VALUES

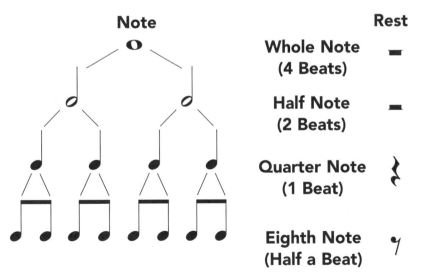

Timing values of three counts and one and a half counts can be represented by dotted notes:

3 counts = 𝅗𝅥.   1 1/2 counts = ♩.

BASS NOTE PICKING

Bass note picking involves a single bass note followed by strumming a chord. Bass notes are generally regarded as being notes on the fourth, fifth and sixth strings.

In this turnaround, the bass notes are played on the first and fourth beats of each bar, and the written chord is strummed on the second and third beats. Even when the single bass note is played, the full chord is held in preparation for the strums to follow; e.g. in the first bar hold a C chord for all four counts.

13.0

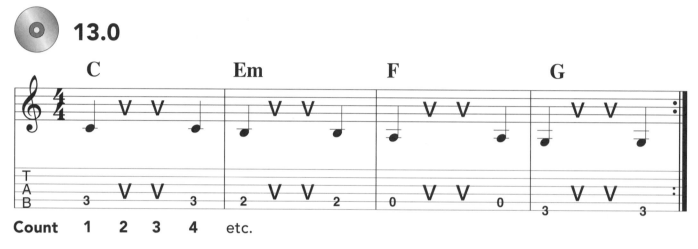

In the following example a bass note is picked on the first and third beats. This 'pick-strum' method of playing is very common in 'country flavoured' songs. You will notice that the bass notes alternate between 2 strings for each chord.

13.1

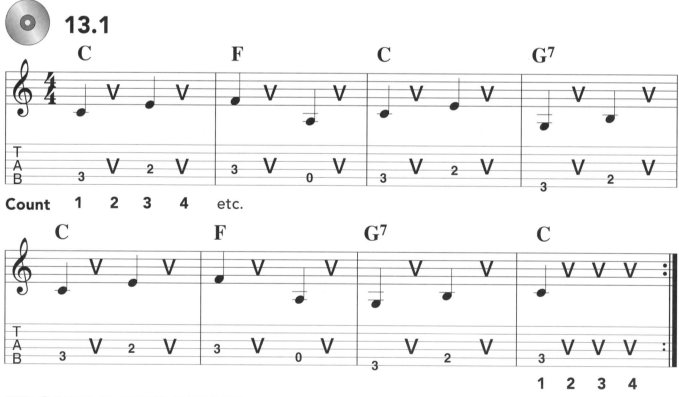

TROUBLE-SHOOTING

1. Fingers on their tips (this is particularly important in bass note picking styles).
2. Continual revision of all notes and chords (at least once a week you should go back through all the lessons).
3. Watch timing and tap your foot with the beat, for both chord and note work.
4. Finish chord progressions on a single strum of the opening chord (this will apply in most situations).

LESSON TWELVE

THE TIME SIGNATURE

A time signature consists of two numbers, which indicate the number of beats per bar and the value of each beat.

$\frac{4}{}$ - this represents 4/1, which indicates the number of beats per bar.

$\frac{}{4}$ - this represents 1/4, which indicates that the beats are quarter notes (crotchets).

$\frac{4}{4}$ time is also referred to as 'Common Time' which is represented by a '**C**'.

Most rock songs are in $\frac{4}{4}$ time

$\frac{3}{4}$ TIME

Many popular songs are written in $\frac{3}{4}$ time. This is often called 'Waltz Time' and indicates 3 quarter note beats per bar. Accent (play louder) the first beat.

Play each rhythm pattern two times and end each by a single strum of the C major chord.

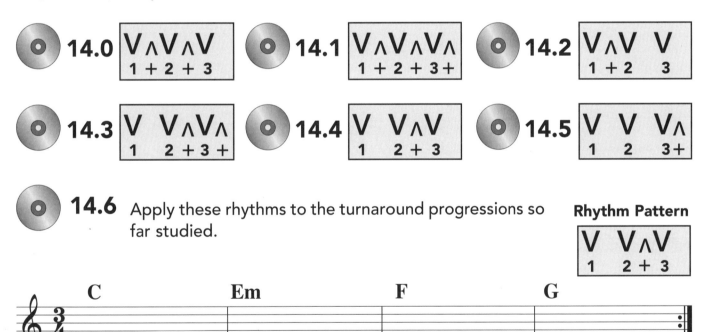

14.6 Apply these rhythms to the turnaround progressions so far studied.

BASS NOTE PICKING ($\frac{3}{4}$ TIME)

15. The progression below combines an alternating bass with a 2 bar rhythm.

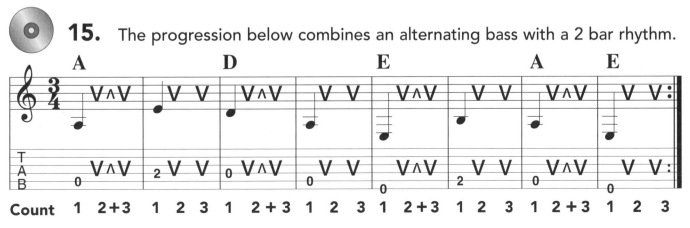

LESSON THIRTEEN

CHORDS A MINOR AND D MINOR

The following progression uses the above chords, and is played in $\frac{3}{4}$ time. Count in groups of three and accent the first beat.

16.0

V	V ∧ V ∧
1	2 + 3

```
       C              Am             Dm             G7
 &  3                                                      
    4                                                      
```

BASS NOTE RUNS

A bass note run is a series of single notes played on the bass strings. They are used to connect two chords, adding interest to a given progression.

A combination of bass note runs and bass note picking can be applied to the new progression introduced above. For example:

16.1

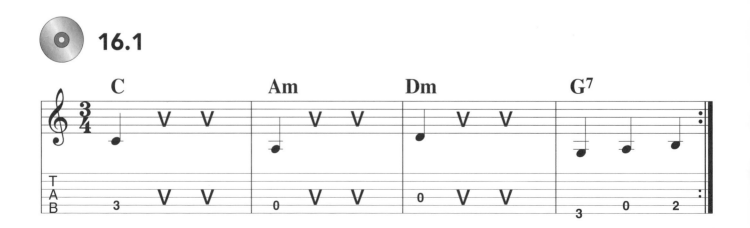

LESSON FOURTEEN

CHORDS C MAJOR 7 AND F MAJOR 7

Do not confuse the major 7 chord (e.g. C major 7, written above as 'Cmaj7') with the dominant 7 chord (e.g. C dominant 7th, written as 'C7').

SIXTEENTH NOTE RHYTHM PATTERN

In musical notation, a sixteenth note has the value of half an eighth note and is indicated as such ♬ (also called a semiquaver). Thus 2 sixteenth notes equal an eighth note and 4 sixteenth notes equal a quarter note.

Strum equivalent of sixteenth notes are written as such:

Count	V ∧ V ∧
	1 e + a
Say	One ee and ah

The syllables '1 e + a' are used to represent each of the 4 quick strums.

The example below uses the sixteenth note rhythm on the 3rd beat. Play it through twice using a Cmaj7 chord:

17.0

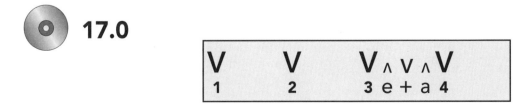

In order to play this rhythm correctly, you will have to keep the beat slow. As the timing is difficult, try clapping the rhythm first.

Apply this new rhythm to the following major 7th chord progression:

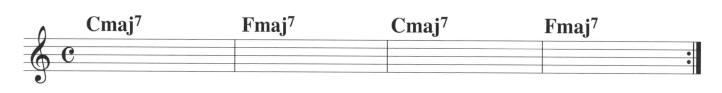

17.1

TROUBLE-SHOOTING

1. Observe the time signature of a progression before you commence playing.
2. Tap you foot with the beat only (especially with sixteenth note rhythms).
3. Make full use of pivot and slide techniques.
4. Memorize chord shapes as they are introduced and do not confuse dominant 7 with major 7 chords.
5. Practice playing songs from sheet music.

LESSON FIFTEEN

CHORDS, A MAJOR 7, D MAJOR 7 AND G MAJOR 7

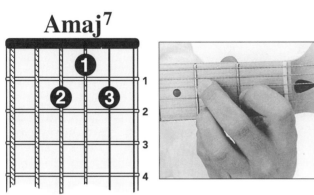

Amaj⁷

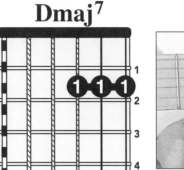

Dmaj⁷

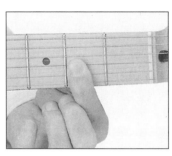

A cross placed above a string indicates that its sound is to be 'deadened.' This deadened sound is achieved by touching the string without applying pressure. In the Gmaj7 chord the 5th string is deadened by the second finger, as shown in the photo:

Gmaj⁷

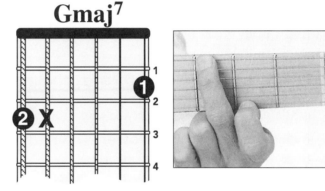

MAJOR 7 PROGRESSION

Play this progression using the following 2 bar rhythm pattern. Make full use of slide and pivot fingers.

Rhythm Pattern

V ∧ V ∧ V	V V ∧ V
1 + 2 + 3	1 2 + 3

⌐— First Bar —⌐ ⌐—Second Bar—⌐

18.

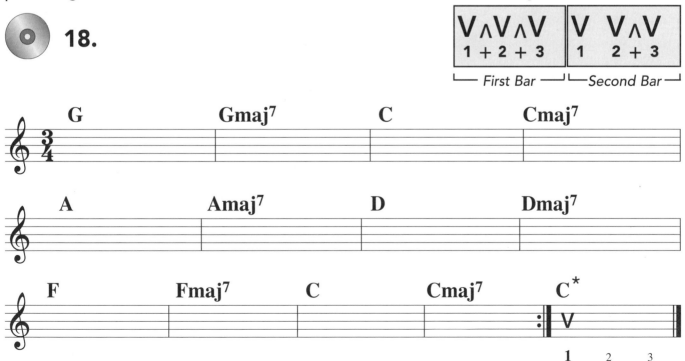

* In the last bar of this example, the C chord is played only on the first beat, and then held for the remaining two beats, as indicated by the count.

THE CHROMATIC SCALE

A scale can be defined as a series of notes in alphabetical order, going from any one note to its octave. Each scale is based upon a set pattern. In Lesson Ten you were introduced to the notes of the musical alphabet set out as such:

In this scale, B to C and E to F were said to be a semitone apart, with all other notes being a tone apart. In the chromatic scale, however, all notes are separated by a semitone, giving the following pattern:

The new notes that the chromatic scale introduces are called sharps and flats.

♯ indicates a sharp, which raises the pitch of a note by one semitone. (see fretboard diagram)

♭ indicates a flat, which lowers the pitch of a note by one semitone.

Thus it is possible for the same notes to have two different names. (e.g. F sharp has the same position on the fretboard as G flat). Below is a representation of the chromatic scale on the fretboard.

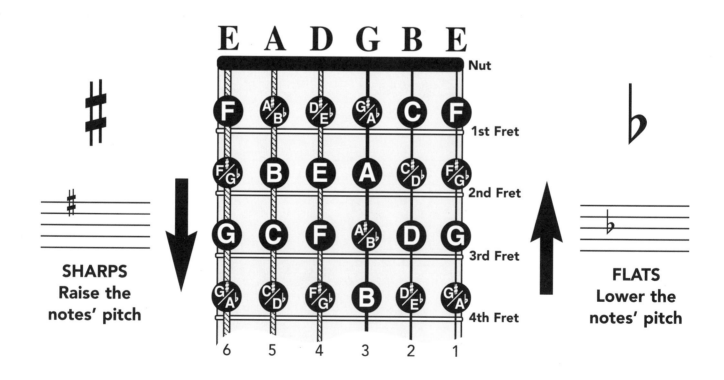

SHARPS
Raise the notes' pitch

FLATS
Lower the notes' pitch

LESSON SIXTEEN

CHROMATIC NOTE SUMMARY: FIRST POSITION

In music notation, sharps and flats are placed in front of the notes they affect; e.g. F sharp is written on the staff thus: -

The sharp or flat sign must be placed on the same line or space as the note.
Here is the full range of notes in the first position, including all sharps and flats.

For the relative positions of these notes on the fretboard, refer back to the fretboard diagram on the previous page. The notes marked in brackets are called **enharmonic notes** because they have the same pitch, but different names; e.g. A♯ and B♭ have the same position on the fretboard, but different positions on the staff.

PROGRESSION IN A

The following progression uses chromatic notes as part of the bass note runs in bars 2 and 6.

19.

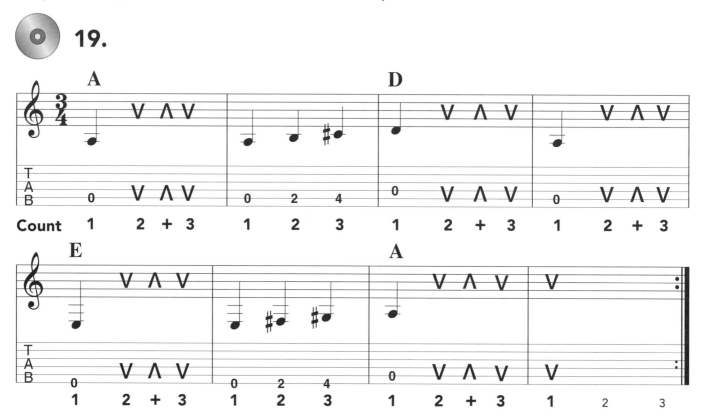

In the last bar of this example, the A chord is played only on the first beat, and then held for the remaining two beats, as indicated by the count.

EXPERIMENTS IN BASS NOTE PICKING

In the following progression, the bass notes have been left out intentionally, so that you may experiment with your own combinations. Bass notes are to be played on the first and fourth beats, with strums on the second and third beats. There are two main rules governing the choice of bass note to be used: -

1. They must be chosen from notes on the fourth, fifth and sixth strings (the bass strings).
2. They must only be selected from notes found in the chord (as written next to each chord).*

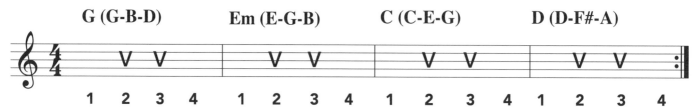

Theoretically, there are many possible combinations of bass note picking with this example. However, you must take into consideration the overall sound since some of the combinations will sound better than others.

* Do not confuse bass note picking with bass note runs, which may use notes not found in the chords.

LESSON SEVENTEEN

B MINOR CHORD

Bm

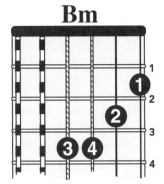

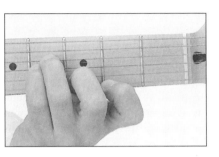

Both the fifth and sixth strings are not played in this Bm chord.
Try Turnaround No. 2 in the key of G:

20.0

Rhythm Pattern

V	V	∧	V	∧	V	∧
1	2	+	3	+	4	+

G	Bm	C	D

Unlike 12 bar blues, where the progression occurs over a fixed number of bars, the turnaround progression may vary in length. In the example above, turnaround 2 occurs over six bars; notice however, that the chord sequence remains the same (thus it is the sequence, not the length, that makes a progression a turnaround).

TRIPLET RHYTHM

In triplet rhythms, three evenly spaced strums are played in each beat. This is best illustrated by the following example. Play it twice through using a B minor chord:

20.1

ACCENT

Rhythm Pattern

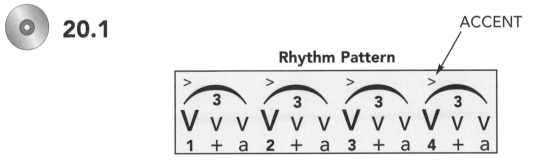

Keep the beat (represented by the foot tapping) very slow, and make sure that the foot taps with the beat, not with the number of strums played. There are twelve strums per bar, but only four beats. You should accent (play louder) each strum that occurs on the beat (indicated by the arrowhead).

Apply the triplet rhythm to Turnaround No. 2 in G; using all down strums.

20.2

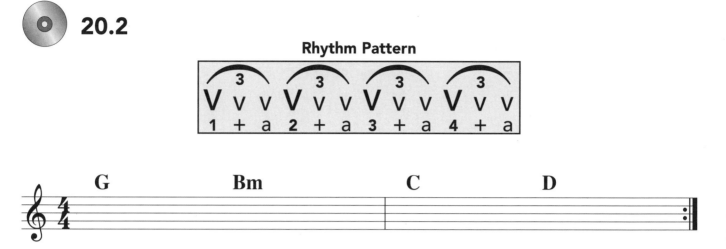

In this example, each chord is played for two beats (i.e. 6 strums). The overall 'feel' of the triplet rhythm is that of a fast waltz.

TURNAROUND NO. 1 IN D

The introduction of the Bm chord now enables you to play Turnaround 1 in the key of D.

20.3

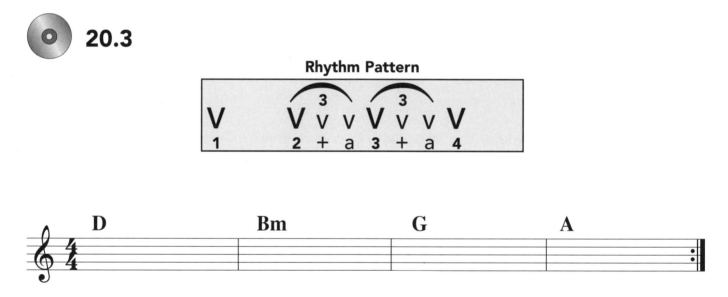

This rhythm pattern combines the triplet strum (2nd and 3rd beats) with the basic down strum (1st and 4th beats).

LESSON EIGHTEEN

CHORDS E6 AND A6

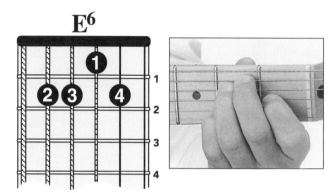

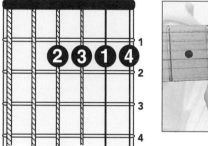 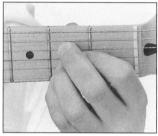

An alternative fingering for this chord is to bar across all 4 strings with the first finger.

BLUES IN E

The 12 bar blues below combines major chords, sixth chords and seventh chords. When changing from the sixth chord to the seventh chord, the little finger utilises the sliding technique introduced in Lesson 3. This technique is essential to make the sixth to seventh chord changes sound smooth.

21.

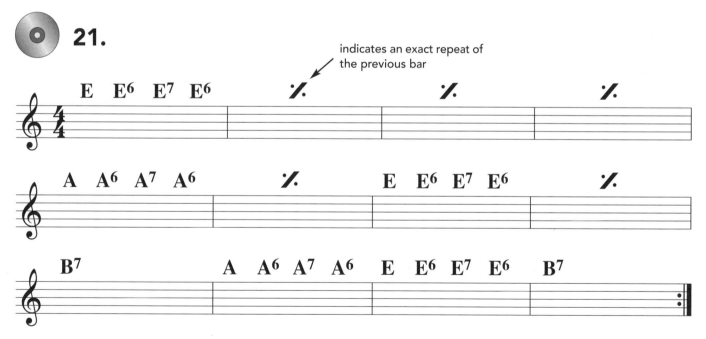

Except for the two bars of B7, you are changing chords on every beat (i.e. 4 chord changes per bar). This will be difficult, so use an easy rhythm; e.g.

Rhythm Pattern

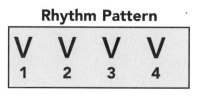

THE MAJOR SCALE

In Lesson Fifteen a scale was defined as being a set pattern of notes, in alphabetical order, going from any note to its octave. The most common scale in music is called the major (or ionian) scale, which is identified by the familiar sound:

Play these notes:

C MAJOR SCALE

The C major scale can be written on the staff as such:

22.

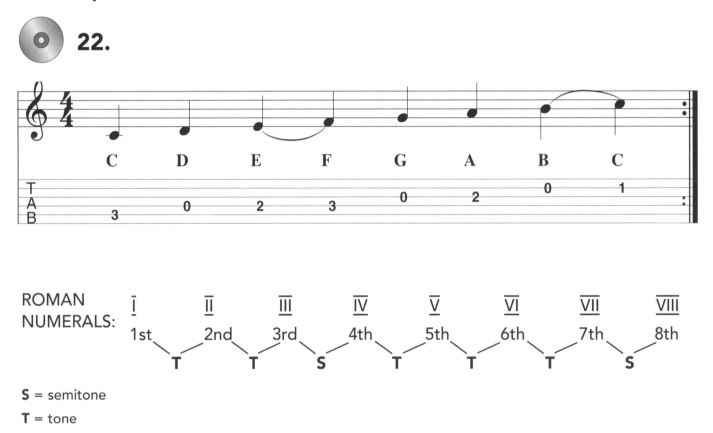

ROMAN NUMERALS:

I	II	III	IV	V	VI	VII	VIII
1st	2nd	3rd	4th	5th	6th	7th	8th
	T	T	S	T	T	T	S

S = semitone

T = tone

Each note of the scale can be identified by using Roman numerals. Thus F is said to be the 4th of the C scale, G is the 5th and so on.*

You will notice that between the 3rd-4th and the 7th-8th notes there is only a distance of one fret (i.e. a semitone, indicated by the curved line. All other notes are separated by one tone (2 frets). This pattern of notes and semitones remains the same for every major scale (which will be explored in more detail when other major scales are introduced.

* This Roman numeral representation can also be applied to chords and chord progressions.

LESSON NINETEEN

'ROCK CHORDS'

In Lesson One a chord was defined as being a group of 3 or more notes; however, rock guitarists often use a technique of strumming only 2 strings of a chord. Although this is theoretically not a chord, it shall be referred to as one. The following 'rock chords' (also called power chords) involve playing the 5th and 4th strings only.

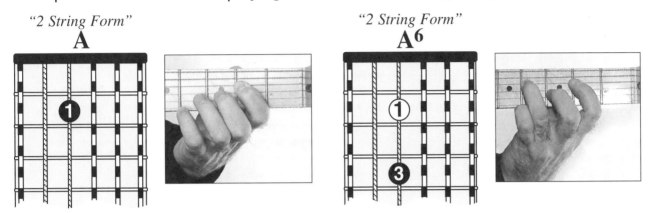

Try the following example, using both A and A6 chords, 2 string form.

23.0

Repeat this example until you are familiar with its sound, remembering that the first finger must remain in position at all times, even when the A6 chord is being played, (as indicated by the open circle). To get the correct sound both the 5th and 4th strings must be strummed together. Do not use the 4th finger for the A6 chord.

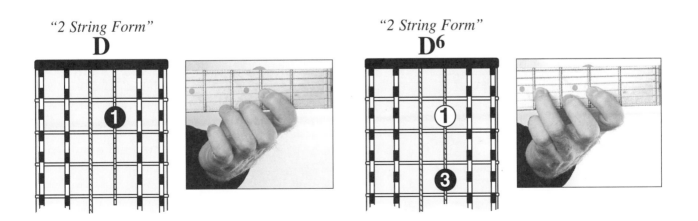

44

This D chord shapes shown on the previous page are the same as the A chord shapes, but moved across one string. Here is the same example as before, but this time using D and D6 chords.

Once again, be sure only to play 2 strings (the 4th and the 3rd strings). Avoid hitting the 5th or 6th strings.

The E chord shape is played using the 6th and 5th strings, as such:

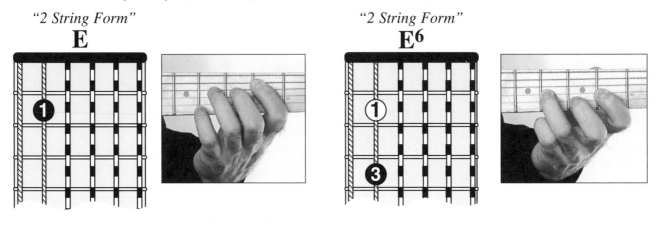

 **23.2**

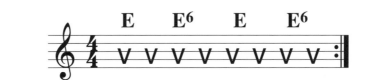

12 BAR IN A

The 2 string rock chords that you have been studying are used in many 12 bar songs. Consider the following blues in A.

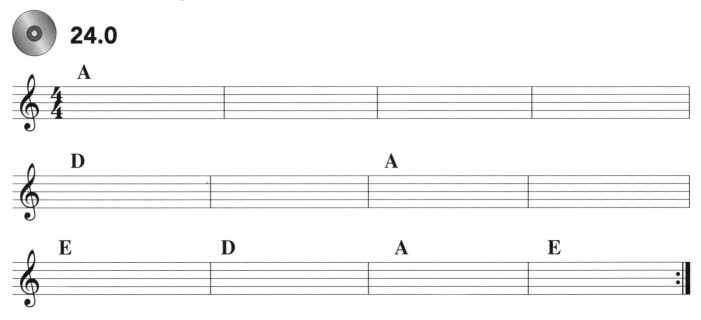

In this 12 bar pattern for each bar of A play:

A   A6   A   A6

V V V V V V V V
1 + 2 + 3 + 4 +

for D play:

D   D6   D   D6

V V V V V V V V
1 + 2 + 3 + 4 +

and for E play:

E   E6   E   E6

V V V V V V V V
1 + 2 + 3 + 4 +

'ROCK CHORD' VARIATION

Try the following rock chord variation against the 12 bar blues in A.

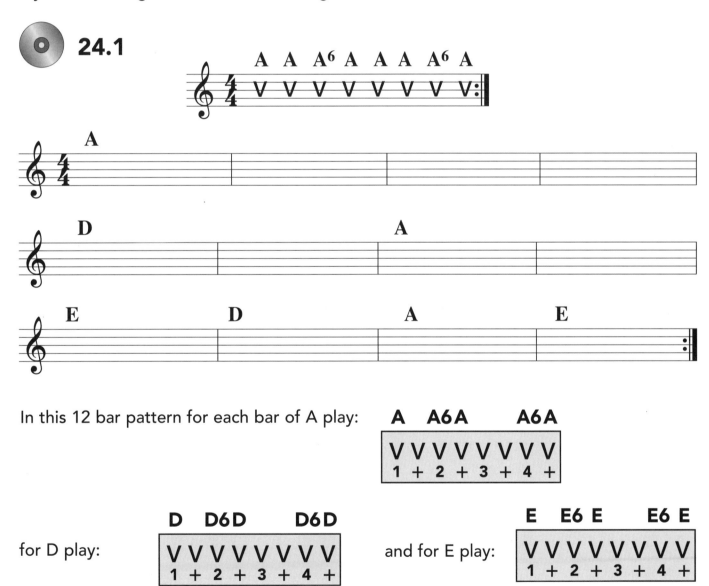

In this 12 bar pattern for each bar of A play:

A   A6 A   A6 A

V V V V V V V V
1 + 2 + 3 + 4 +

for D play:

D   D6 D   D6 D

V V V V V V V V
1 + 2 + 3 + 4 +

and for E play:

E   E6 E   E6 E

V V V V V V V V
1 + 2 + 3 + 4 +

LESSON TWENTY

SUSPENDED CHORDS: A SUS, D SUS AND E SUS

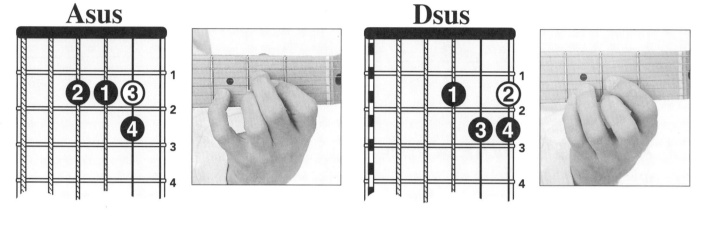

Asus

Dsus

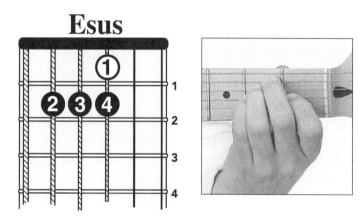

Esus

In sheet music the suspended chord is often written as 'sus4' e.g. 'Asus' and 'Asus4' are the same chord. Suspended chords are often used in conjunction with major chords to add interest to a progression, as illustrated in the following example. The sus chords are played on the up stroke of the 2nd beat in each bar.

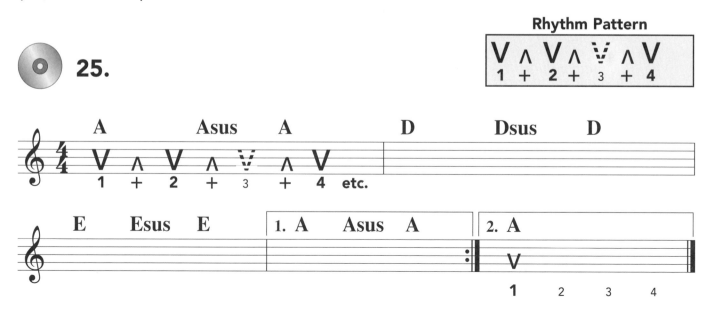

25.

Rhythm Pattern

V ∧ V ∧ V ∧ V
1 + 2 + 3 + 4

G MAJOR SCALE

From Lesson 10, a major scale can be represented by Roman numerals as such:

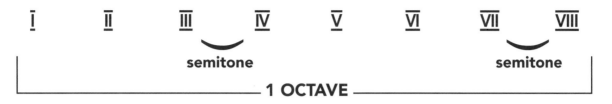

I represents the first note of the scale, called the root (or key) note, e.g. in the C major scale C is the root note. In the G major scale, G is the root note, i.e.:

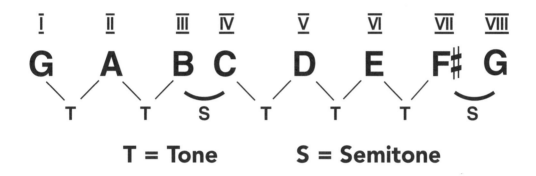

By definition, for this major scale to have the correct sound, the 3rd-4th notes and 7th-8th notes should be separated by only one semitone. F♯ must therefore be used to comply with the correct sequence, i.e. a tone between the 6th-7th notes and a semitone between the 7th and 8th notes.

26.

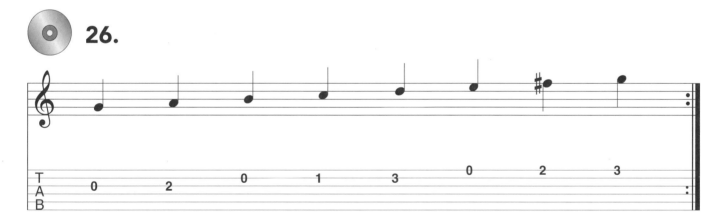

Play up and down this G scale slowly, listening for the major scale sound (Do, Re, Mi etc.)

LESSON TWENTY ONE

THE HAMMER ON

A 'hammer on' refers to the technique of sounding a note without actually picking the string with the pick. The sound is produced by striking the string with one of the left hand fingers. To play a hammer on, first hold an Am chord:

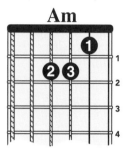

Keeping the first and third fingers in position, lift the second finger off the fourth string. Pick the open fourth string, then bring the second finger down firmly and quickly to its position on the second fret, (an E note) without picking the string again. This action should produce the E note quite clearly. After this hammer on has been completed strum the Am chord.

In music notation, what you have just played is written as in Example 27.0: The hammer on effect is indicated by the curved line, and the small 'H' between the two notes in question. Remember that the second note (E) is not picked; the sound is produced entirely by the second finger 'hammering' on to the string.

The hammer on is most effective when used in conjunction with strumming and bass note picking. You must be very careful with the timing of the hammer on. Both the D and E notes are eighth notes and each should have equal time value when played (regardless of the hammer on technique).

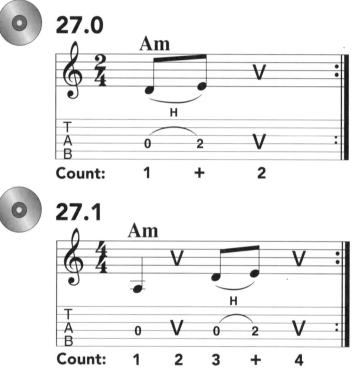

The hammer on is an extremely popular technique which can be played with virtually any chord shape. It can also be played with any finger holding a note of the chord. For Am you could hammer on with the first or third fingers as such:

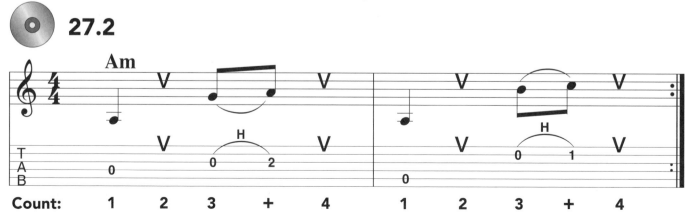

The combinations of hammer on, bass note picking and bass note runs are virtually endless, so you should experiment as much as possible.

HAMMER ON EXAMPLES

In order to play the following progression smoothly, you should practice each chord section individually.

27.3

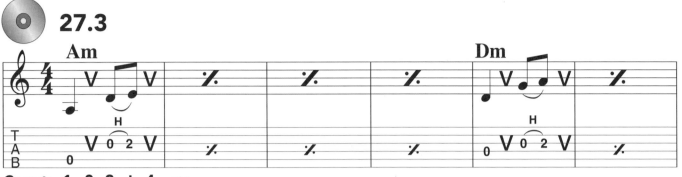

Count: 1 2 3 + 4 etc.

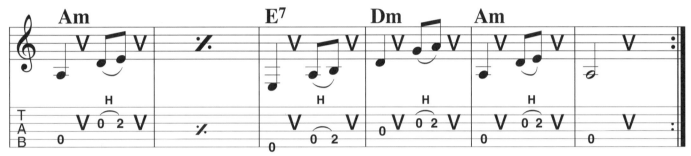

THE PULL OFF

The pull off is a technique often used in conjunction with the hammer on. It involves the finger flicking the string as it pulls away from it, creating the sound of the note.
The pull off is indicated by the curved line, and the small 'P.'

Here is an example, using the G chord:

In this example the hammer on and pull off are played on the 3rd beat. This involves the use of triplet notes (indicated by a curved line and a 3), which have the same timing as that of the triplet rhythm, introduced in Lesson 17.

28.0

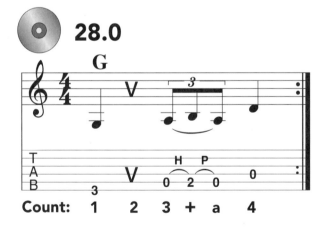

Count: 1   2   3 + a   4

Remember to actually pull the string as you pull your finger away, as opposed to just lifting the finger off the string. Try the following example, involving hammer ons, pull offs and triplet notes.

28.1

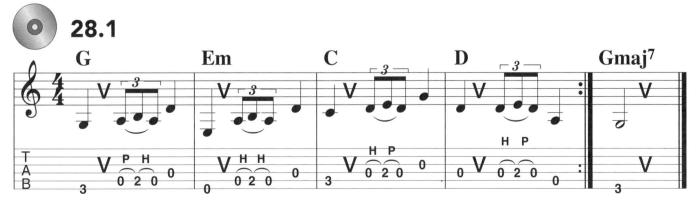

SECTION ONE SUMMARY

You have now completed the first section of this book, and written below is a summary of what has been studied. You should revise the contents of this list thoroughly before commencing Section Two

CHORDS: A, Am, A7, A6, Amaj7, Asus, Bm, B7, C, C7, Cmaj7, D, Dm, D7, Dmaj7, Dsus, E, Em, E6, E7, Esus, F, Fmaj7, G, G7, Gmaj7.

RHYTHMS:

V	V ∧	V V V	V∧V∧
1	**1 +**	**1 + a**	**1 e + a**
one strum per beat	two strums per beat	three strums per beat	four strums per beat

TECHNIQUES: Bass note picking. Bass note runs. The hammer on. The pull off.

THEORY: Basic musical terms (i.e. Staff, Treble Clef, Bar, Bar line, etc.)
Notes in the open position.
Time signatures: $\frac{3}{4}$ and $\frac{4}{4}$
Chromatic scale.
Major scale.

EXTRA PROGRESSIONS

The following extra progressions will add variety and further use of the chords, rhythms and techniques studied in Section One.

29. Progression 1

Rhythm Pattern

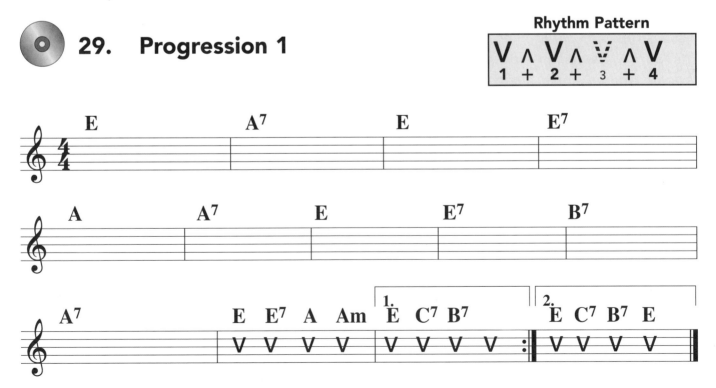

30. Progression 2

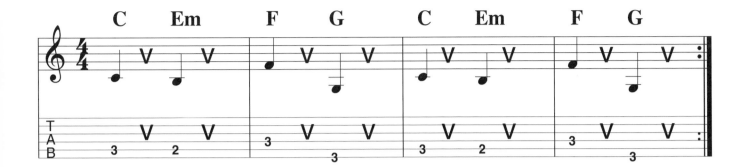

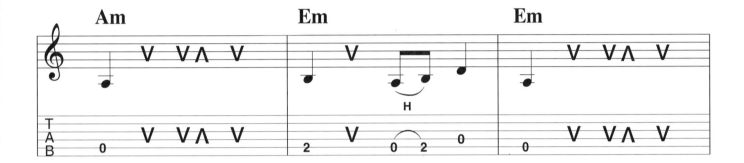

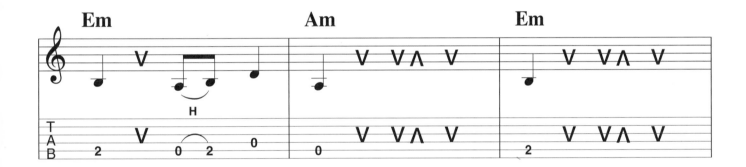

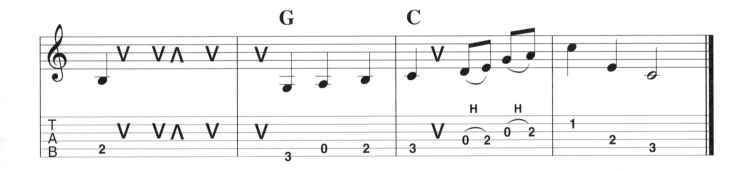

31. **Progression 3**

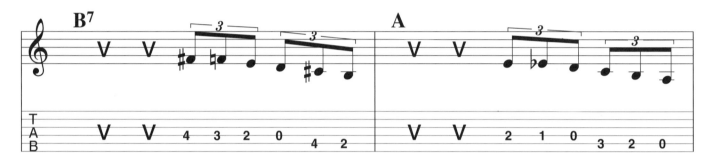

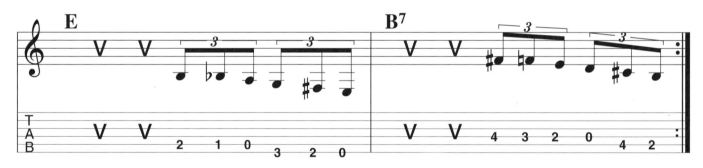

32. **Progression 4**

SECTION TWO

LESSON TWENTY TWO

THE BAR CHORD

Up to this point, all the chords you have studied are referred to as 'open chords' i.e. they contain at least one open string. A bar chord, however, has no open strings, due to the fact that the first finger 'bars' across all six stings. This is illustrated with the F major chord below:

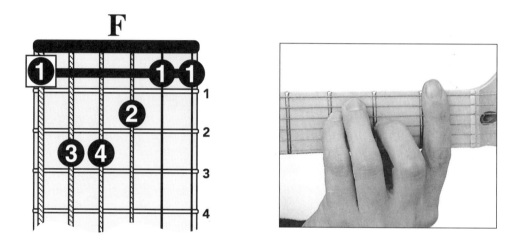

In playing this chord, the first finger holds down all six strings, while the second, third and fourth fingers hold an E major chord shape (see photo). Strum the F chord, and concentrate on producing a clear sound from all six strings. As with the open chords, bar chords will be difficult in the early stages and will need much practice.

ROOT 6 BAR CHORD

From the photo above, you can see that the F major chord is actually an open E major chord moved up one fret, with the first finger replacing the nut. The root note (the note after which the chord is named, i.e. F), can be found on the sixth string; hence the name 'Root 6 bar chord' *. When this chord shape is moved up and down the fretboard its name changes but the basic shape does not. The chord's name is taken from the note on the sixth string, (i.e. the root note) so you must become thoroughly familiar with all of these notes.

* Root 6 bar chords can also be called E formation bar chords, because they are based upon an E chord shape.

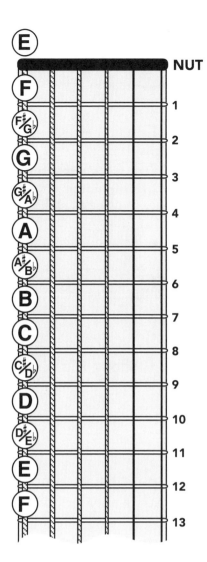

At the third fret, the root 6 bar chord shape becomes a G chord.

At the fifth fret, the root 6 bar chord shape becomes an A chord.

By following through this procedure, the root 6 bar chord gives you at least 8 major chords, some of which are completely new to you (e.g. F♯ on the second fret, A♭ on the fourth fret, etc.)*. The actual number of bar chords you can play will depend on the type of guitar you have. If you have a classical guitar, you may only be able to bar up to the eighth fret, whereas on an electric guitar you should be able to play up to the 12th fret.

ROOT 6 BAR CHORD PROGRESSION

Rhythm Pattern

V	V	V	V
1	2	3	4

🖸 **33.0**

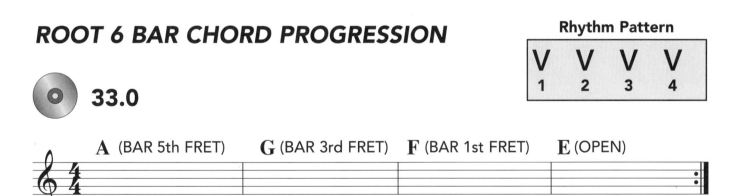

In this example a slide technique is used when changing from one chords to the next. This technique involves the fingers releasing pressure, but not losing contact with the strings during the changes. While changing, the fingers should maintain the basic chord shape. For ease of playing, the open E chord is played using the second, third and fourth fingers. This will enable the slide technique to be used from F to E and E back to A.

* In learning these chords, relate their fret locations to the position marker dots on your guitar.

LESSON TWENTY THREE

PROGRESSION IN F

 **33.1**

A slow beat must be maintained in this progression so that the long slide between F and B flat is achieved without a break in the rhythm.

THE PERCUSSIVE STRUM (Bar Chords)

The technique known as percussive strumming is one of the most common techniques used by rhythm guitarists. Hold an F bar chord shape, but apply no pressure to the strings. Your left hand fingers should be just touching the strings (to deaden them). When you strum the strings the resulting sound is known as a percussive strum.

A percussive strum is indicated by a cross placed above the wedge mark, as illustrated in the following example, with percussive strums on the second and fourth beats.

33.2

Rhythm Pattern

```
      X         X
V ∧ V     V ∧ V
1 + 2     3   4
```

Apply this rhythm to the progression in F above.

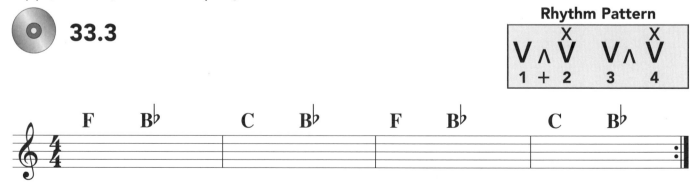

33.3

THE PERCUSSIVE STRUM (Open Chords)

The percussive strum technique introduced above can also be applied to open chords. With open chords the deadening is achieved by releasing pressure on the fretted notes and tilting the left hand (see photograph below) to cover the other open strings.

C chord before deadening

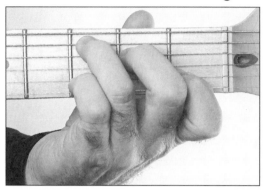

C chord after deadening

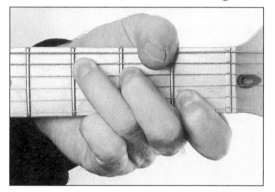

The thumb is used to
deaden the sixth string.

Try the following example:

Rhythm Pattern

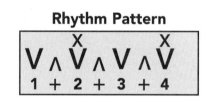

 **34.**

LESSON TWENTY FOUR

BAR CHORD PROGRESSION

The following chord progression utilises the percussive strum technique in association with root 6 bar chords.

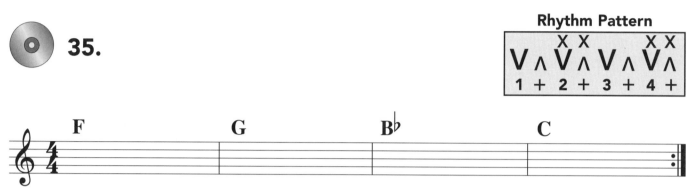

As rhythms become more advanced it will be necessary for you to practice each chord progression and its rhythm pattern separately (i.e. practice the chords using an easy rhythm and then practice the given rhythm using just one chord). This should be done thoroughly before combining the two.

KEY SIGNATURES

Melodies of songs are constructed from notes within a given scale. Occasionally 'outside' notes are used, but generally most notes in a melody will come from within the scale; e.g. a melody in the key of C major will use the notes from the scale of C.

C D E F G A B C

A melody in the key of G major will use the notes from the G scale:

G A B C D E F♯ G

where F sharp will occur rather than F natural.* Instead of placing a sharp sign in front of every F note, a key signature is used. Every major scale has a different key signature which shows the number of sharps or flats contained within the scale. The key signature is written at the beginning of each stave of music (directly after the treble clef). For the key of G major, a sharp sign is written on the F line, indicating that all F notes are to be played as F sharp:

Therefore, the key signature of G major contains one sharp, F sharp.

The C major scale contains no sharps or flats, hence the key signature will also contain no sharps or flats, and is represented thus:

* A natural note is a note that is neither sharpened nor flattened. Natural signs (♮) are used in music to cancel the effect of a sharp or a flat.

LESSON TWENTY FIVE

ROOT 6 MINOR BAR CHORD

Fm

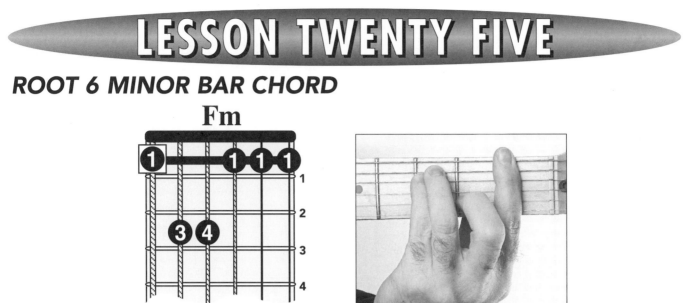

The F minor bar chord is actually an open E minor chord moved up one fret, with the first finger barring across the first fret. This minor chord can be formed from the root 6 major bar chord by simply lifting off the second finger. Like the major chord, the basic shape can be moved up and down the fretboard; its name once again being taken from the 6th string note, e.g. Fm on the first fret, Gm on the third fret, Am on the fifth fret and so on.

MINOR BAR CHORD PROGRESSIONS

36.

Rhythm Pattern

V	V v v V	V
1	2 + a 3	4

A (5th FRET)   F#m (2nd FRET)   Bm (7th FRET)   E (OPEN)

This rhythm uses a triplet strum on the second beat. Refer back to Lesson Seventeen to refresh your memory on the triplet strum, remembering that your foot taps only with the beat and that the triplet rhythm uses all down strums.

37.

Rhythm Pattern

V ∧ V ∧ V ∧ V
1 + 2 + 3 + 4

E (OPEN)   G#m (4th FRET)   F#m (2nd FRET)   B (7th FRET)

The suggested rhythm above is a variation of the basic down/up pattern introduced in Lesson Eight. There is a down strum played away from the guitar on the second and third beats. Continuous right hand movement must be maintained.

LESSON TWENTY SIX

TWO BAR PERCUSSIVE RHYTHM

The following percussive rhythm is commonly used by rock guitarists:

38.0   **Am** (Bar chord)

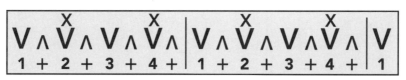

Try this rhythm with the following chord progression; using bar chords.

38.1

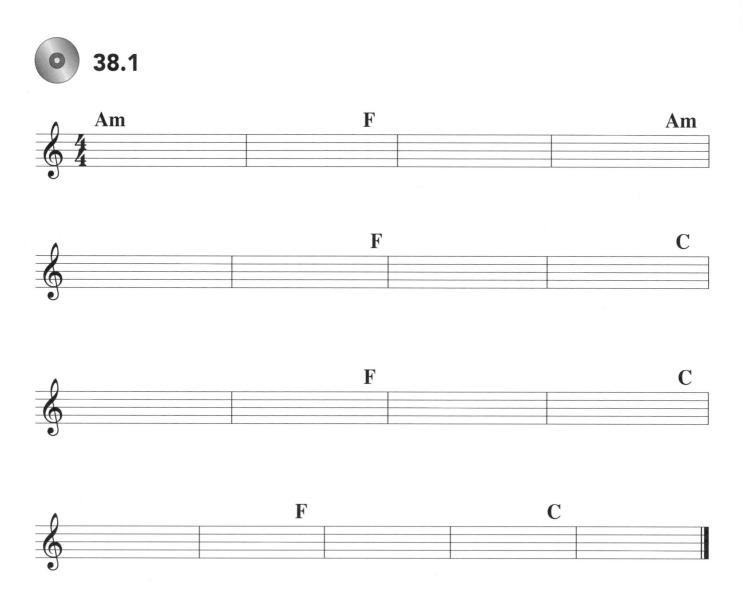

Notice that the chord change (from Am to F and F to C) is on the 'and' section of the 4th beat.

SUMMARY OF SCALES AND KEY SIGNATURES

Each major key has a specific number of sharps or flats contained in its key signature. Listed below are 8 scales (together with their key signature), which are the most commonly used in sheet music and general playing.

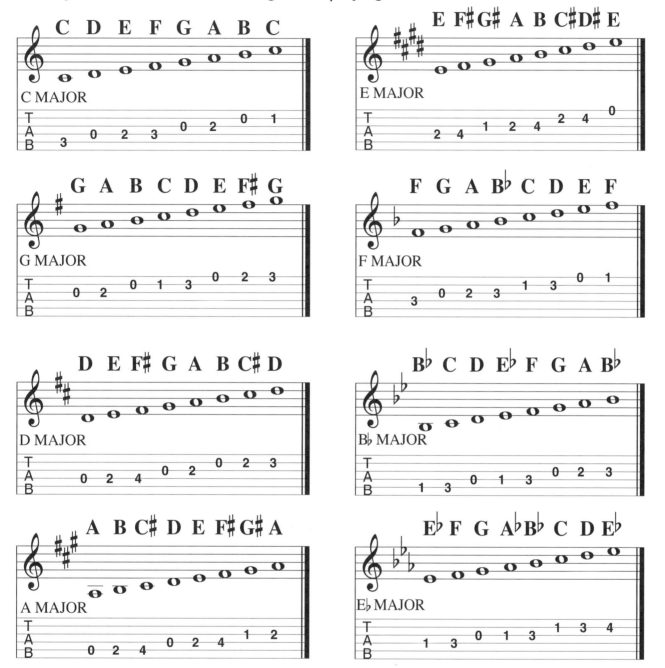

A summary of the above scales is outlined in the table below. Make a special effort to memorize these key signatures.

KEY	SHARPS	KEY	FLATS
C	-	C	-
G	F♯	F	B♭
D	F♯, C♯	B♭	B♭, E♭
A	F♯, C♯, G♯	E♭	B♭, E♭, A♭
E	F♯, C♯, G♯, D♯		

DOMINANT 7TH BAR CHORD (ROOT 6)

F⁷

The 7th chord can be formed by holding a root 6 major bar chord and moving the fourth finger to the second string, as shown in the photo above. The F7 is a difficult chord to finger because of the stretch required to cover four frets, but as you move down the fretboard (to B♭7 and C7 shown below) the fingering becomes easier.

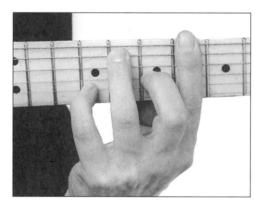

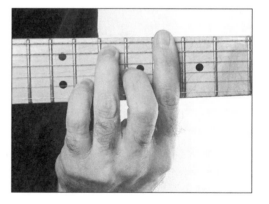

* An alternative shape for the dominant 7th root 6 bar chord is:

F⁷

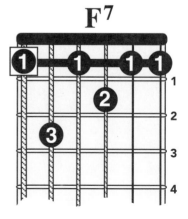

* This chord shape is based on the alternative E7 chord introduced in Lesson Eleven.

The following example uses the root 6 major and seventh bar chords.

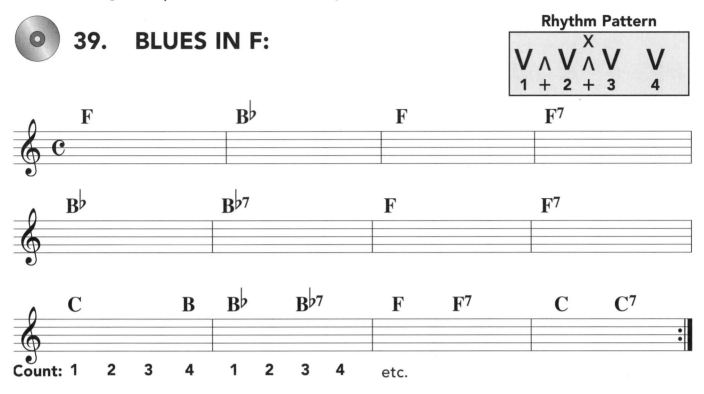

39. BLUES IN F:

Rhythm Pattern

This 12 bar pattern substitutes the $\overline{IV}$ chord (B♭) in the second bar for the $\overline{I}$ chord (F). This is common practice that can be applied to all previous 12 bar blues to add variety. In bars 9 to 10 a passing chord principle is used. The basic progression is C to B♭, however the passing chord B is used on the last beat of the 9th bar. As a general rule, any two chords that are one tone apart can be connected by moving the chord shape in semitones. The passing chord will usually occur on only one beat, for example:

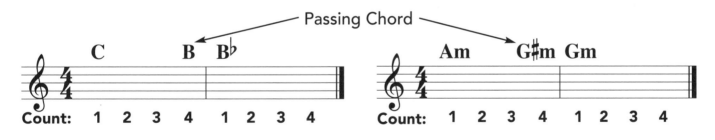

RESTS IN MUSIC

A rest in music represents a period of silence. For every note value there is an equivalent rest value; this can be summarized in the following table:

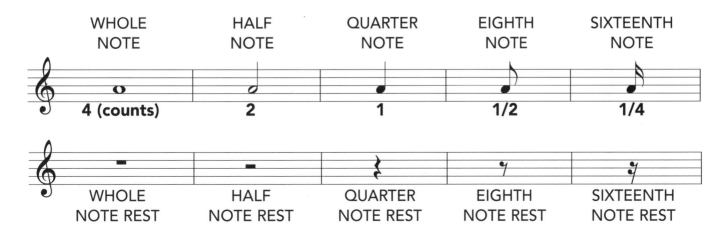

WHOLE NOTE	HALF NOTE	QUARTER NOTE	EIGHTH NOTE	SIXTEENTH NOTE
4 (counts)	2	1	1/2	1/4
WHOLE NOTE REST	HALF NOTE REST	QUARTER NOTE REST	EIGHTH NOTE REST	SIXTEENTH NOTE REST

LESSON TWENTY EIGHT

RIGHT HAND DEADENING TECHNIQUE

In chord playing, rests are achieved by deadening the strings with the right hand. Hold an open A chord and strum all 6 strings, then, without releasing left hand pressure, deaden all the strings with the side of your right hand palm, as illustrated in the photographs below. This deadening should be done on the next beat.

Apply the following rhythm pattern to the progression below using a basic A chord. Play it very slowly at first. Play it twice through.

Rhythm Pattern

40.0

V	𝄽	𝄽	V
1	2	3	4

40.1

OPEN CHORDS

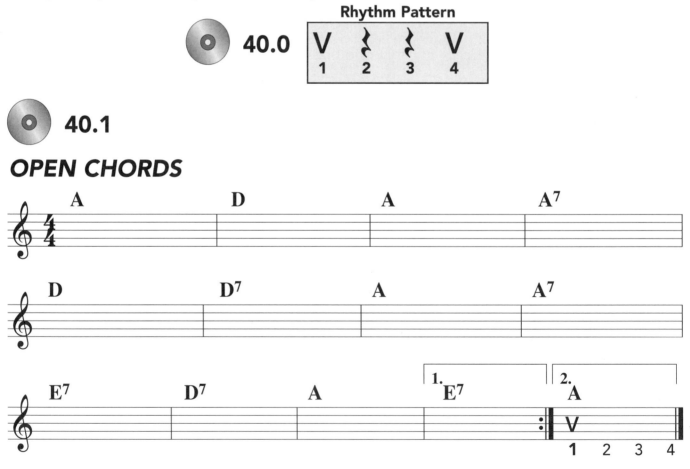

Strum chords on the first and fourth beats; deaden chords (with the right hand) on the second beat (which is also held for the third beat).

This right hand deadening technique should also be applied to bar chord progressions. Try the new rhythm with the following turnaround in the key of C (using bar chords).

41.0

BAR CHORDS

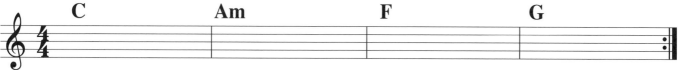

Make sure that you deaden the strings with the right hand and not with the left hand (by releasing pressure on the chord shape).

Now try the following rhythm variation, playing it through twice:

41.1

41.2

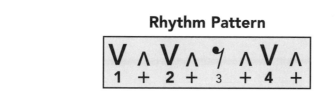

EIGHTH NOTE RESTS

Play the following rhythm, as studied in Lesson Eight:

Rhythm Pattern

V	∧	V	∧	V	∧	V	∧
1	+	2	+	3	+	4	+

Instead of holding the chord shape on the '3' count, use an eighth note rest. This will involve the right hand deadening technique. Play it through twice:

42.0

Rhythm Pattern

V	∧	V	∧	↿	∧	V	∧
1	+	2	+	3	+	4	+

42.1   Apply this rhythm to the following example.

LESSON TWENTY NINE

STACCATO STRUMMING

A further application of the right hand deadening is used in staccato strumming. 'Staccato' means to cut short, and a staccato strum is indicated by a dot placed above the wedge mark, as shown in example 43.0.

Strum a Gmaj7 chord (open) and immediately after strumming, deaden the strings with the right hand. Play it through twice.

 43.0

Rhythm Pattern

V̇   V̇   V̇   V̇
1   2   3   4

Unlike the example in the last lesson, where the deadening occurred **on** the beat, in staccato strumming, the deadening occurs immediately after the strum - **before** the next beat. In the example below, the Gmaj7 chord is strummed on the first beat and is deadened immediately after; creating a definite period of silence before the second beat.

 43.1

V̇   V̇ ∧ V ∧ V̇   V̇
1   2 e + a 3   4

Apply this new rhythm to the following open chord progression.

43.2

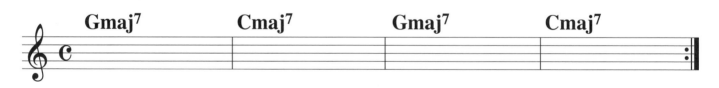

Gmaj⁷   Cmaj⁷   Gmaj⁷   Cmaj⁷

When the staccato technique is being played correctly, the right hand motion involves a rapid flicking of the wrist in order to cut the strum very short. Try this new rhythm with the following bar chord progression.

44.

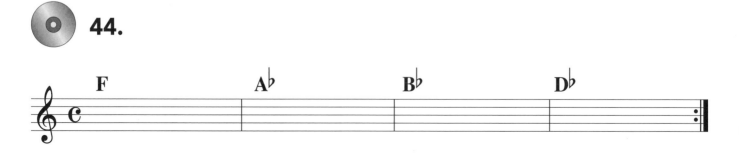

F   A♭   B♭   D♭

LESSON THIRTY

ROOT 5 BAR CHORD

The three bar chord shapes you have so far studied (major, minor and dominant 7th) have all had their root note on the sixth string. Bar chords with their root note on the fifth string shall now be studied. As with the root 6 chords, you will need to become familiar with the notes on the fifth string in order to name each root 5 bar chord. These chords can also be called 'A formation' bar chords.

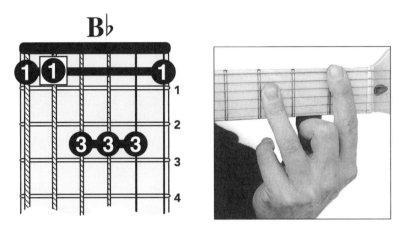

B♭

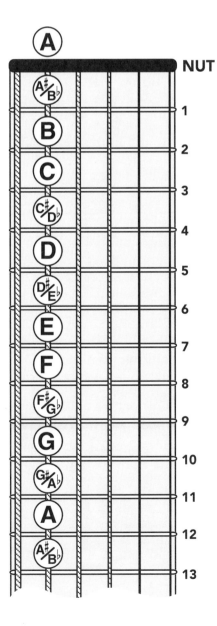

This B♭ major bar chord can be regarded as an open A shape moved up one fret. However, instead of using three fingers, as is the case with the open A chord, the third finger is used to bar all three notes (see photo).

At the third fret, the root 5 bar chord shape becomes a C chord, at the 5th fret it becomes a D chord, at the 7th fret it becomes an E chord, and so on.

The root 5 major chord shape is perhaps the most difficult one you have studied so far. It will take much patience and perseverance to master. The main problem that you may encounter is accidental deadening of the first string with the third finger. The ability to overcome this depends on the flexibility of the last finger joint of the third finger. It is essential to produce a clear sound from the remaining five strings, even if the first string is deadened.

12 BAR IN G

This 12 bar blues uses a combination of root 6 and root 5 bar chords.

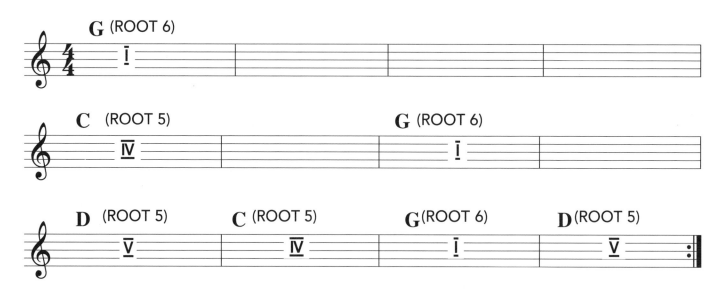

Underneath each chord, Roman numerals (as illustrated in Lesson 10) have been written to indicate the basic chords used in 12 bar progressions. The resulting pattern can be set out thus:

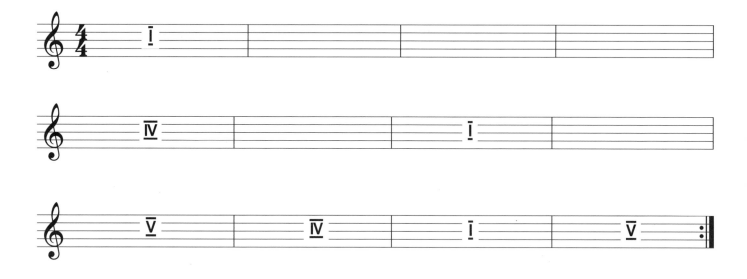

It is important for you to remember that 12 bar in any key uses the three chords, Ī, IV and V.

LESSON THIRTY ONE

BASIC PATTERNS

As a competent rhythm guitarist you will need to be able to play the 12 bar blues progression in any key. From the last lesson, the chords to be used for 12 bar are the Ī, ĪV and V̄. As bar chords, these chords form definite patterns on the fretboard, which can be moved up and down, enabling you to play in any key. (This process of changing keys is called **transposition***).

Consider a blues in G, using all root 6 bar chords. The three chords, G, C and D (Ī, ĪV, and V̄) are found at the 3rd, 8th and 10th frets respectively. The pattern formed by these chords can be summarized thus:

BLUES PATTERN NO. 1

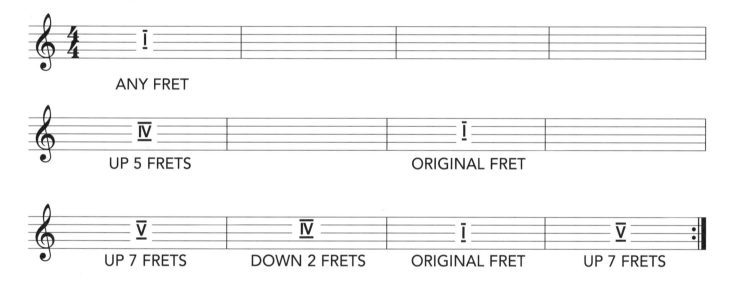

This pattern is most convenient for the keys of E, F, G♭, G, A♭ and A.

Another basic pattern involves the use of both root 6 and root 5 bar chords. Using the key of G as an example once again, the three chords, G, C and D are located at the 3rd, 3rd and 5th frets respectively (see last lesson's blues). The basic pattern for these chords is on the following page.

* See Appendix 3.

BLUES PATTERN NO. 2 (using root 6 and root 5 bar chords).

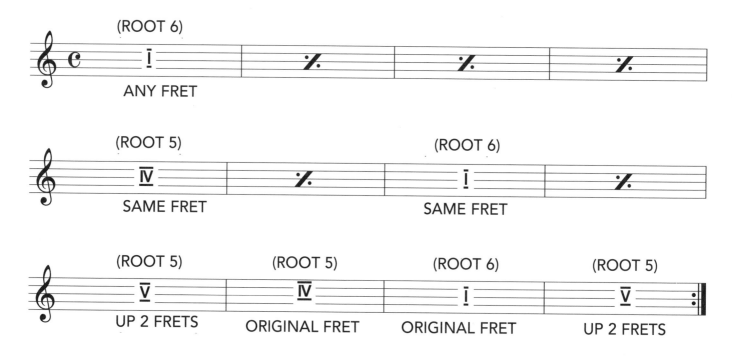

This pattern is most convenient for the keys between F and C.

By using basic patterns such as these, you will only need to locate the root 6 position of the Ī chord in order to play the whole 12 bar progression.

Practice playing 12 bar as much as possible, using the 2 patterns so far described (you will be working in the keys of E to C). This is an ideal opportunity to revise all rhythms studied to date.

LESSON THIRTY TWO

DAMPENING TECHNIQUE

A 'dampened' sound can be created by resting the right hand on the strings while strumming. This sound can only be achieved by placing the right hand close to the bridge, as illustrated in the photographs below.

In rhythm notation, the dampening technique is indicated by a small D placed above the strum symbol, as shown in the example below.

The dampening technique is often used in conjunction with bar chords, playing only two bass strings. For root 6 bar chords, play the 6th and 5th strings, and for root 5 bar chords, play the 5th and 4th strings.

Hold a G bar chord and apply the dampening technique technique as such:

 45.0

G (Bar chord)

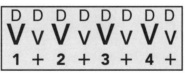

Try the following progression using the above rhythm. You will notice that the F sharp and B are passing chords, played only on the 'and' portion of the 4th beat.

45.1

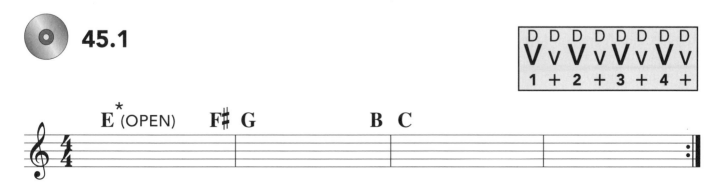

* For the open E chord, play only the 6th and 5th strings.

LESSON THIRTY THREE

'ROCK CHORDS'

In Lesson 11 you were introduced to 'rock chords' as used in 12 bar blues. The same principle can now be applied to bar chords. Using root 6 bar chords, the G and G6 'rock chords' are played with the following fingering*.

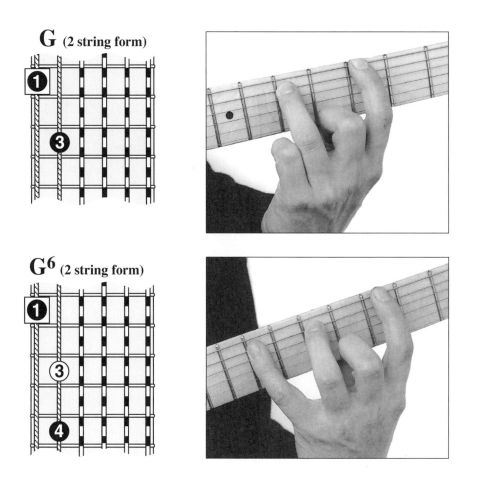

* An alternative fingering used by many rock guitarists for these chords is as such:

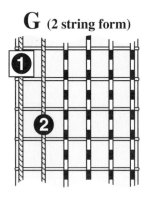 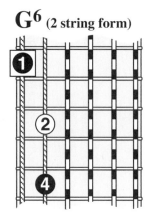

These 'rock chord' shapes can be regarded as root 6 chords because G and G6 are at the 3rd fret; C and C6 are at the 8th fret; and D and D6 are at the 10th fret.

46.

Play a blues in G, using these chords, and the same rhythm pattern used in Lesson 19 (example 24.1).

Rhythm Pattern

G	G	G6	G	G	G	G6	G
V	v	V	v	V	v	V	v
1	+	2	+	3	+	4	+

BLUES PATTERN NO. 3

The 2 blues patterns studied on pags 69 and 70 enabled you to play blues in the keys of E to C. For the remaining keys (D flat, D and E flat), these two patterns become awkward to play, hence a third pattern is commonly used. This pattern starts on a root 5 bar chord:

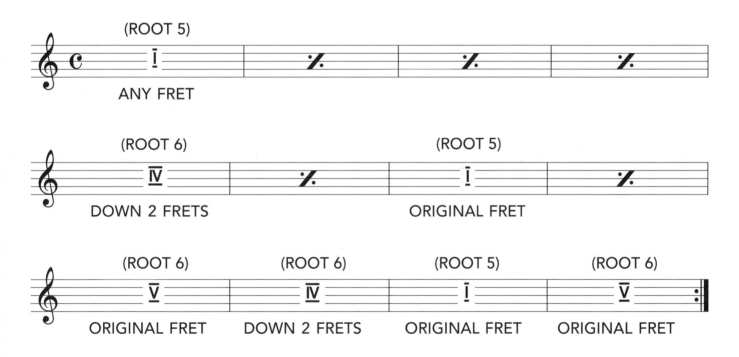

This pattern can be used for the keys C to G. To be a versatile rhythm guitarist you must be able to play 12 bar blues in any key, and the 3 basic patterns now enable you to do so. Written below is a summary of these keys that best suit each pattern.

PATTERN	KEYS
1	E - A
2	F - C
3	C - G

Where the keys overlap, either pattern can be used.

ROOT 5 MINOR BAR CHORD

B♭m

The root 5 minor bar chord is derived from the open A minor shape. Try the following example:

47.0 The suggested rhythm is a sixteenth note strum as introduced on page 35.

Rhythm Pattern

V ∧	V ∧	V ∧	V ∧ V
1 +	2 +	3 +	4 e + a

B (ROOT 6)	**D♯m** (ROOT 5)	**A** (ROOT 6)	**C♯m** (ROOT 5)

G (ROOT 6)	**Bm** (ROOT 5)	**F♯7** (ROOT 6)	**B** (ROOT 5)

ROOT 5 MINOR BAR CHORD PROGRESSION

47.1 The rhythm used in this progression involves a percussive strum on the '2' and '4' counts.

Rhythm Pattern

V	V ∧ V	V ∧
1	2 + 3	4 +

Em (ROOT 5)	**D** (ROOT 5)	(ROOT 5) **C**

	Bm (ROOT 5)	**Em**

LESSON THIRTY FIVE

A BASIC TURNAROUND PATTERNS

In Lessons Thirty One and Thirty Three you were introduced to three basic patterns for the blues progression. These patterns enable you to play a blues in any key. The same principle of basic patterns can be used in turnarounds. Consider turnarounds 1 and 2 in the key of A:

TURNAROUND 1

BASIC PATTERN ONE (Starting on a root 6 bar chord)

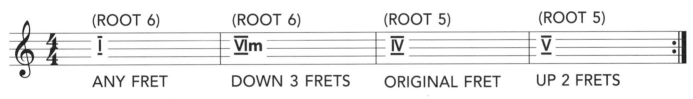

BASIC PATTERN TWO (Starting on a root 5 bar chord)

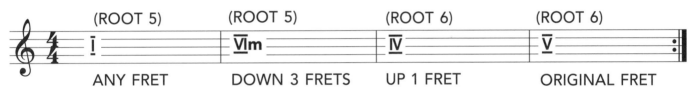

TURNAROUND 2

BASIC PATTERN THREE (Starting on a root 6 bar chord)

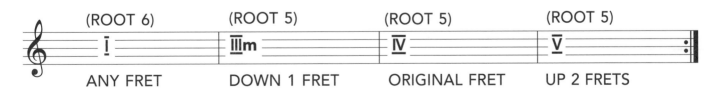

BASIC PATTERN FOUR (Starting on a root 5 bar chord)

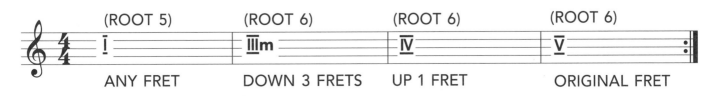

There are two patterns for each turnaround, enabling you to play them in any key. Here is a summary of the keys in which each pattern may be used:

PATTERN 1	G to D	TURNAROUND 1
PATTERN 2	C to F	TURNAROUND 1
PATTERN 3	F to D	TURNAROUND 2
PATTERN 4	C to F	TURNAROUND 2

You should practice turnarounds in all keys (some examples shown below), using different rhythms. Try some of the songs listed in Appendix Two.

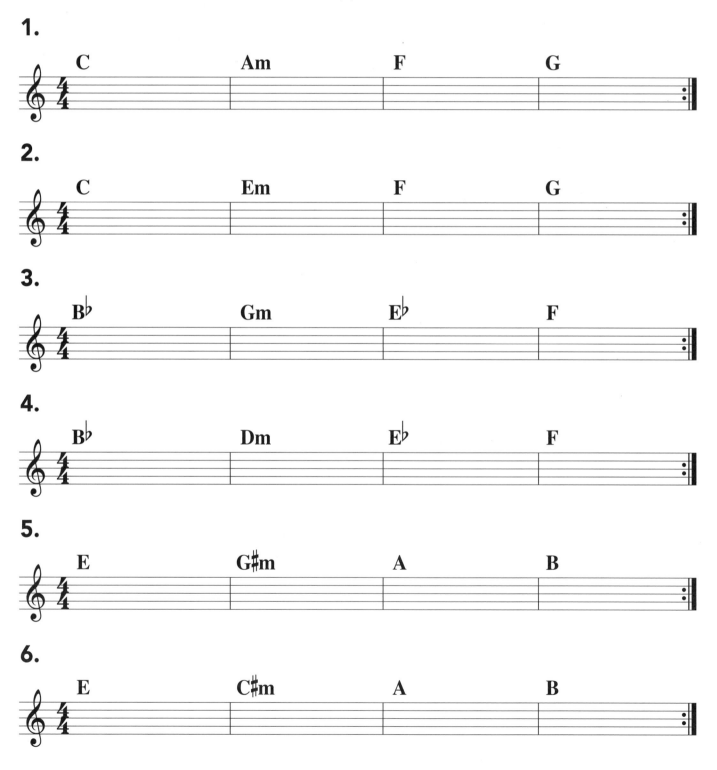

LESSON THIRTY SIX

RIGHT HAND RHYTHM TECHNIQUE

The right hand techniques of staccato strumming (Lesson Twenty Nine) and dampening (Lesson Thirty Two) can be combined to create some very popular and interesting rhythms. Try the following rhythms, using the dampening technique on the '1+' and '3+' beats, and a staccato up strum on the 2nd and 4th beats. When playing the staccato up strum, only hit the first and second strings.

48.0

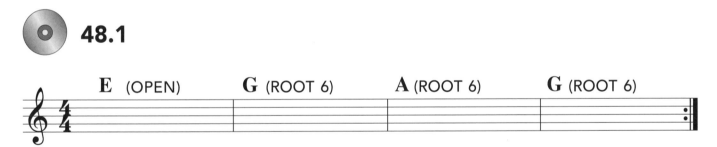

Apply this new rhythm to the following progression:

48.1

E (OPEN)	G (ROOT 6)	A (ROOT 6)	G (ROOT 6)

The same techniques are used in the following variations:

48.2

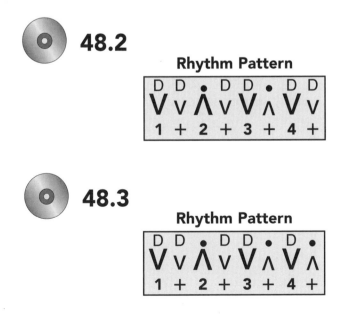

48.3

Remember to hit only the 1st and 2nd strings when playing the staccato up strum.

LEFT AND RIGHT HAND RHYTHM TECHNIQUES

In the following example percussive strums are used, involving the left hand deadening technique.

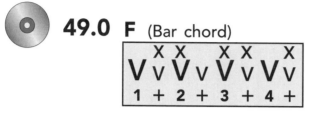

49.0 F (Bar chord)

Apply this rhythm to the following progression, using all root 6 bar chords.

49.1

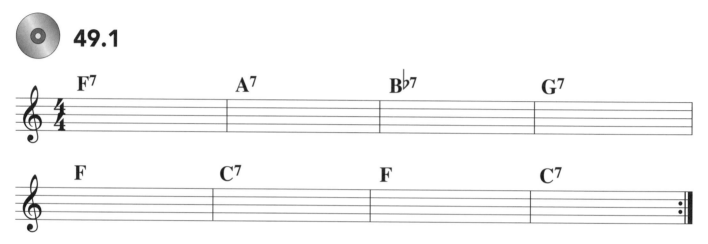

If this rhythm is applied to an open A 'rock chord' the 5th string would be left open, while the 4th string is deadened by the left hand.

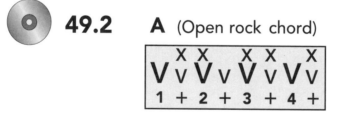

49.2   A (Open rock chord)

The 5th string is referred to as a 'droning' string, with its sound continuously maintained. Play this rhythm with the 12 bar blues outlined in Lesson Eighteen.

The dampening technique (right hand) can also be used in the above rhythm, in place of the percussive strum technique (left hand). This creates a different sound because the A string no longer drones.

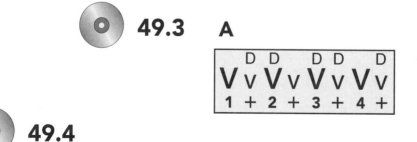

49.3   A

49.4

Apply this rhythm to a 12 bar blues in A (see Lesson 11) using open chords.

CHORD CONSTRUCTION - MAJOR CHORDS

Every chord is based upon a specific formula which relates back to the major scale after which it is named (revise Lesson 14). The formula for a major chord is $\bar{\text{I}}$ - $\overline{\text{III}}$ - $\bar{\text{V}}$, hence the C major chord consists of the first, third and fifth notes of the C major scale, i.e. C - E - G. As you know, a chord must contain at least 3 notes, and any of these three may be repeated. In the open C chord illustrated there are 3 E notes, 2 C notes and 1 G note.

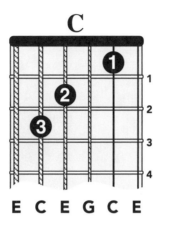

Now consider the D major chord, which is constructed from the D major scale:

D	E	F♯	G	A	B	C♯	D
$\bar{\text{I}}$	$\bar{\text{II}}$	$\overline{\text{III}}$	$\overline{\text{IV}}$	$\bar{\text{V}}$	$\overline{\text{VI}}$	$\overline{\text{VII}}$	$\overline{\text{VIII}}$

The same formula applies ($\bar{\text{I}}$ - $\overline{\text{III}}$ - $\bar{\text{V}}$), so the notes of a D major chord will be D - F♯ - A. (Play an open D chord and check for yourself).

It is important for you to revise all major scales studied so far. Once you have done this, construct the following major chords:

NOTES IN THE CHORD

CHORD	$\bar{\text{I}}$	$\overline{\text{III}}$	$\bar{\text{V}}$
D	D	F♯	A
G			
F			
A			
E			
B♭			

DOMINANT 7TH BAR CHORD - ROOT 5

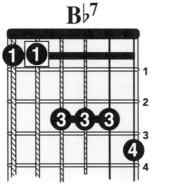

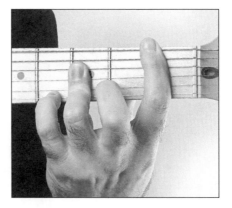

The root 5 dominant 7th bar chord can be formed from the root 5 major shape by adding the little finger, as shown in the photograph. It is a bar chord extension of the open A7 chord. Play the new shape up and down the fretboard, naming each chord as you do so.

BLUES IN G

50.

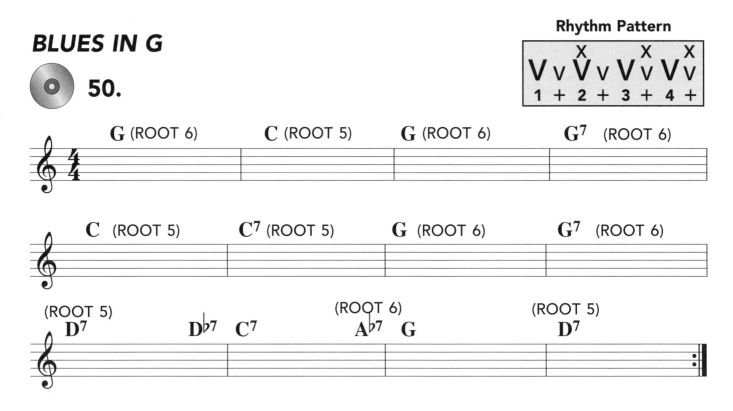

* A common alternative fingering for this chord shape is an extension of the open alternative A7 chord given on page 27.

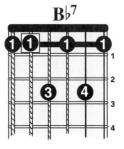

REGGAE RHYTHMS

In ⁴⁄₄ time there is a main accent on the first beat, and a secondary accent on the third beat. To get the feeling of this, you should try counting aloud, and then accent these two beats (i.e. say them louder). This is the usual 'feel' of ⁴⁄₄ time.

Some rhythms, however, have the emphasis placed on the second and fourth beats. These are referred to as 'reggae' rhythms. Consider the pattern below:

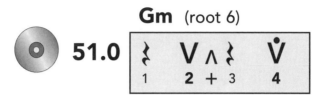

On the third beat the rest is achieved with right hand deadening, and on the 4th beat a staccato strum is played. Try this rhythm with the following progression:

51.1

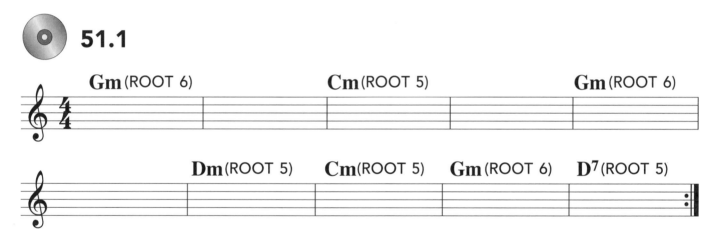

Here is a variation of the reggae rhythm introduced above, using bass note picking on the first beat (as indicated by the note symbol).

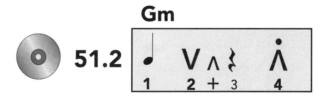

The bass notes played will be on the 6th string for the Gm chord (root 6) and on the 5th string for the Cm, Dm and D7 chords (root 5).

Another variation of this reggae rhythm is to play a percussive strum on the first beat, in place of the bass note.

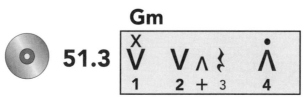

LESSON THIRTY NINE

ARPEGGIO PICKING

Arpeggio picking involves playing chords in single notes rather than strums. For example, hold an open C chord and pick each string in the following order:

52.0

C (open)

String:	5	3	2	1	2	3	5	3	2	1	2	3
Pick motion:	V	V	V	Λ	Λ	Λ	V	V	V	Λ	Λ	Λ
Count:	1	+	a	2	+	a	3	+	a	4	+	a

(Note that a triplet rhythm is being used)

This technique can be applied to either open or bar chords. As a general rule the first note picked (the bass note) will be the root note of the chord, followed by the first three strings as in the order above (3 2 1 2 3). Try the following example, using arpeggio picking and open chord shapes.

52.1

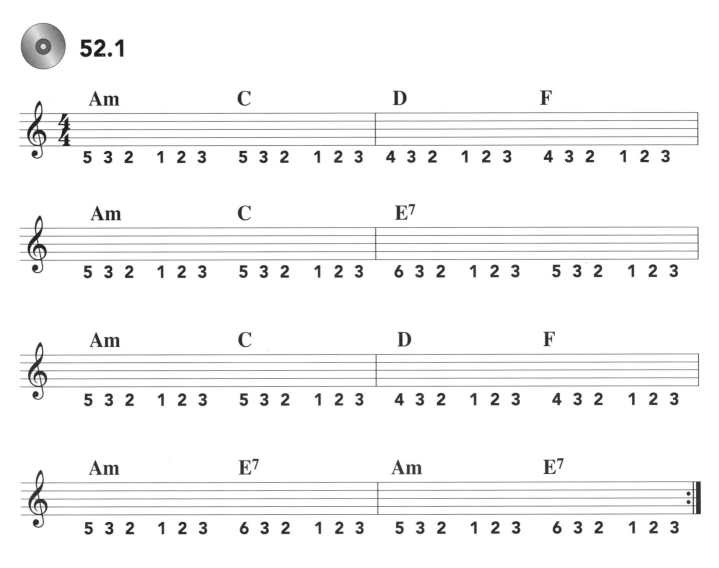

ARPEGGIO VARIATION

Arpeggio patterns can be used in combination with chord strumming. Try the following pattern, using a triplet rhythm:

53.0

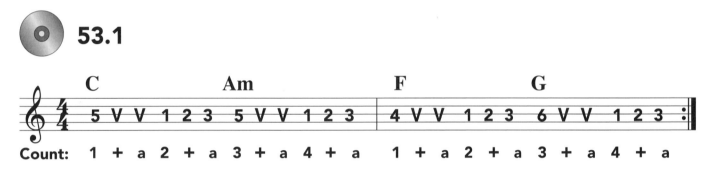

		C (open)										
String:		5	V	V	1	2	3	5	V	V	1	2	3
Pick motion:		V	V	V	Λ	Λ	Λ	V	V	V	Λ	Λ	Λ
Count:		1	+	a	2	+	a	3	+	a	4	+	a

The strums occur on the 'and a' of the first beat. They are preceded by a bass note, and followed by arpeggio picking (on the second beat). Try this new pattern with a turnaround in C using open chords.

53.1

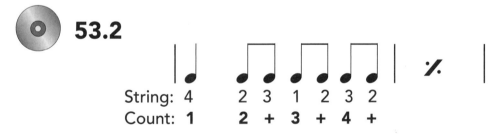

Here is another arpeggio variation.

53.2

String: 4   2 3 1 2 3 2
Count: 1   2 + 3 + 4 +

Apply this variation to the following chord progression. The bass note used should be the root note of the chord. Use open chords.

53.3

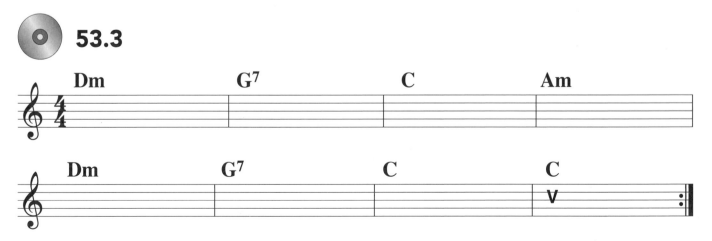

Create your own arpeggio variation and apply them to any progression in this book.

LESSON FORTY

ARPEGGIO PICKING WITH BASS NOTE RUNS

The following example uses a combination of arpeggio picking and bass note runs. The arpeggio picking pattern involves playing the root note, followed by the strings in a set order: 3 2 1 2 3 (as studied on page 82). This pattern remains the same for every chord in the example. The bass note runs occur on the 4th beat of each bar.

54.

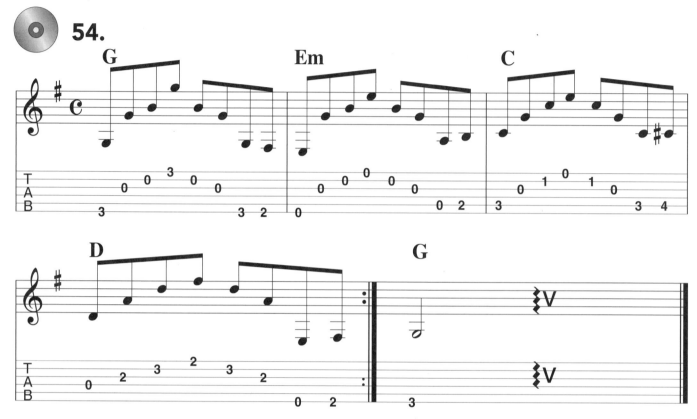

In the last bar, a glide technique on the strum is used, as indicated by the wavy line. This technique involves gliding the pick across all 6 strings, as if strumming slowly.

CHORD CONSTRUCTION - MINOR CHORDS

In Lesson 18 the formula for the major chord was introduced ($\underline{I}$ - $\underline{III}$ - $\underline{V}$). The formula for a minor chord is $\underline{I}$ - $\flat\underline{III}$ - $\underline{V}$. Thus the only difference between a major and a minor chord is the flattened third note; e.g. consider the C and Cm chords:

C:	C	E	G		**Cm:**	C	E$\flat$	G
	$\underline{I}$	$\underline{III}$	$\underline{V}$			$\underline{I}$	$\flat\underline{III}$	$\underline{V}$

Now, looking at the E major scale:

E	F$\sharp$	G$\sharp$	A	B	C$\sharp$	D$\sharp$	E
$\underline{I}$	$\underline{II}$	$\underline{III}$	$\underline{IV}$	$\underline{V}$	$\underline{VI}$	$\underline{VII}$	$\underline{VIII}$

The E major and E minor chords contain the notes:

E:	E	G$\sharp$	B		**Em:**	E	G	B
	$\underline{I}$	$\underline{III}$	$\underline{V}$			$\underline{I}$	$\underline{III}$	$\underline{V}$

Construct the following minor chords:

Am   Dm   Gm   Fm

LESSON FORTY ONE

MINOR 7TH CHORDS

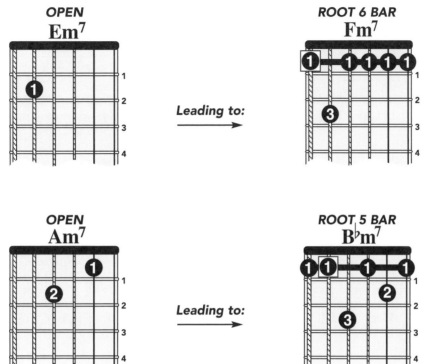

Play the following example, using minor 7th chords:

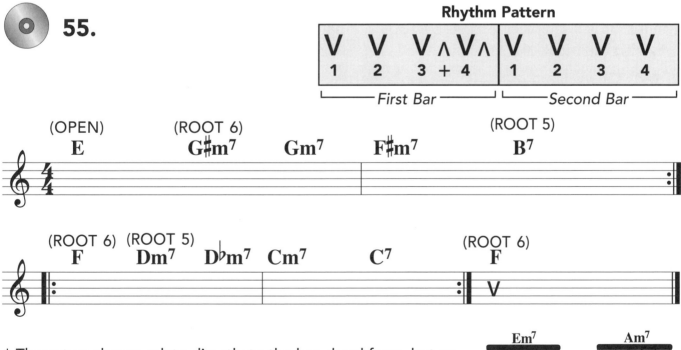

* These two shapes relate directly to the bar chord form, but as open chords the following shapes are more commonly used.

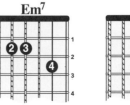

CHORD CONSTRUCTION
DOMINANT 7TH AND MINOR 7TH CHORDS

So far you have studied major and minor chord construction. The dominant 7th chord is formed by adding a flattened 7th note to the major chord, i.e. $\underline{I}$ - $\underline{III}$ - $\underline{V}$ - $\flat\underline{VII}$

The addition of this flattened 7th note can be easily seen when comparing the A and A7 chords:

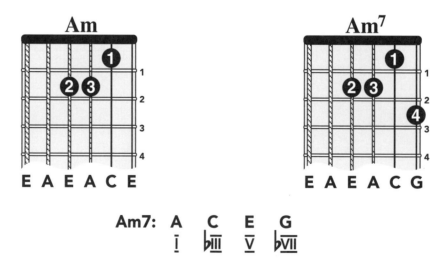

Construct the following dominant 7th chords:

C7   E7   G7   B♭7

Remember to check the sharps of flats involved in each scale when working out the notes of a chord.

The minor 7th chord is formed by adding a flattened 7th to the minor chord, giving the following formula:

$$\underline{I} - \flat\underline{III} - \underline{V} - \flat\underline{VII}$$

The Am7 chord illustrates this:

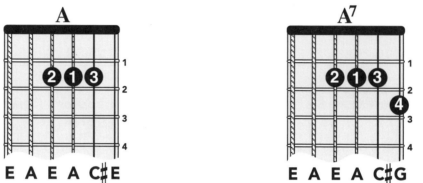

Construct the following minor 7th chords:

Em7   Gm7   Cm7   Fm7

LESSON FORTY TWO

MAJOR 6TH CHORDS

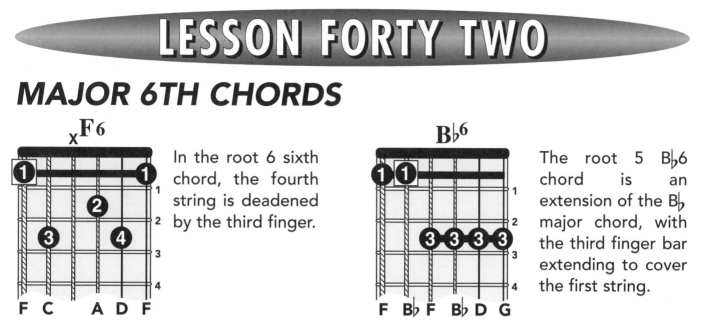

In the root 6 sixth chord, the fourth string is deadened by the third finger.

The root 5 Bb6 chord is an extension of the Bb major chord, with the third finger bar extending to cover the first string.

The formula for a 6th chord is $\bar{I}$ - $\overline{III}$ - $\bar{V}$ - $\overline{VI}$, so the notes contained in the two chords above will be:

F6*:   F   A   C   D
Bb6:   Bb   D   F   G

The following 12 bar blues uses 6th chords in conjunction with major and dominant 7th chords.

56.

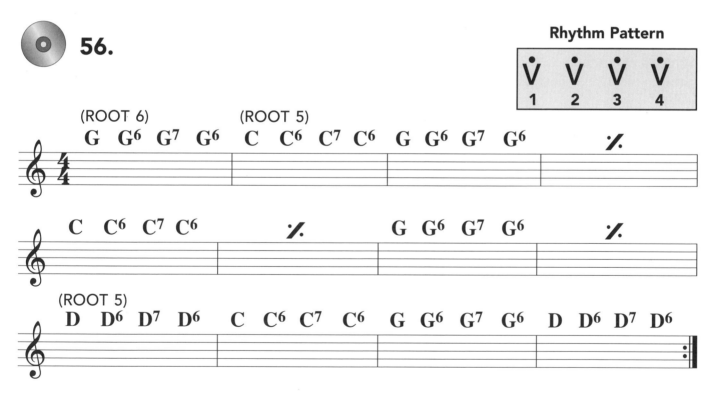

* If you compare the notes of the F6 chord with the notes of a Dm7 chord (see last lesson) you will notice that they are the same, but arranged in a different order:

F6:   F   A   C   D
Dm7:   D   F   A   C

Thus the major 6th and its relative minor 7th are interchangeable (for information on relative minors see Appendix 5).

SEVENTH CHORDS - 'ROCK' FORM

On page 74 you were introduced to two string major and major 6th 'rock chords.' The dominant 7th 'rock chord' can also be used in conjunction with these chords.

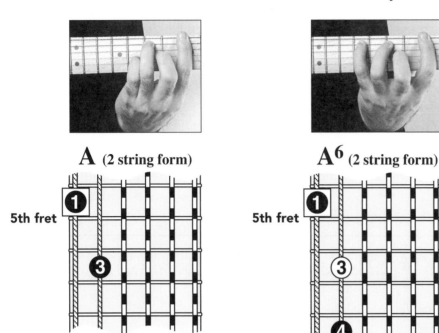

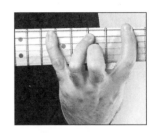

A (2 string form)

5th fret

A⁶ (2 string form)

5th fret

A⁷ (2 string form)

5th fret

A common rock progression uses the above chords as such:

 **57.0**

Rhythm Pattern

A		A6	A	A7	A	A6	A
V	v	V	v	V	v	V	v
1	+	2	+	3	+	4	+

57.1

Apply these chords shapes to a 12 bar blues in A, using blues pattern No.1 (see page 69). The D and E chords use the same shapes at the 10th and 12th frets respectively.

BLUES PATTERN NO. 1

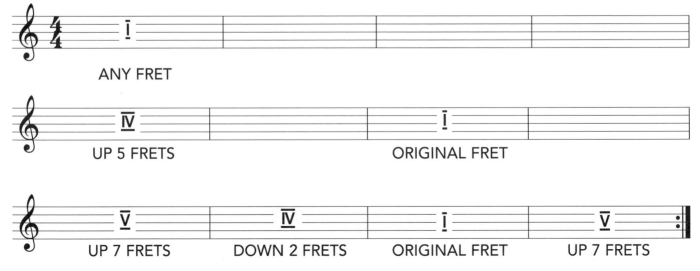

ANY FRET

UP 5 FRETS   ORIGINAL FRET

UP 7 FRETS   DOWN 2 FRETS   ORIGINAL FRET   UP 7 FRETS

LESSON FORTY THREE

ROCK RHYTHM

The following triplet rhythm is commonly used in rock songs. Apply it to the two string rock chords, thus:

58.0

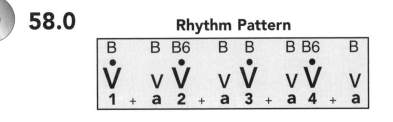

Rhythm Pattern

B		B	B6	B		B		B	B6	B
V̇	v	V̇	v	V̇	v	V̇	v	V̇	v	V
1	+	a	2	+	a	3	+	a	4	+	a

58.1

Now try a blues in B using this rhythm. (Use blues pattern No. 2). For the E and F♯ chords (root 5 bar chords) the two string form involves playing the fourth and fifth strings thus:

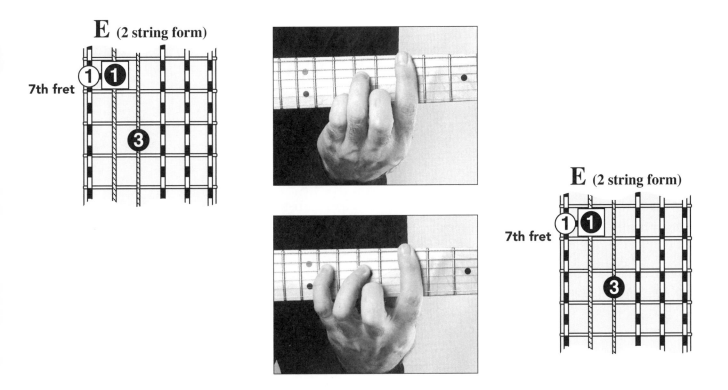

The F♯ major and F♯6 chords use the same shapes at the 9th fret.
This new triplet rhythm should also be applied to the chord progression outlined in the last lesson (Example 57.1)

58.2

Rhythm Pattern

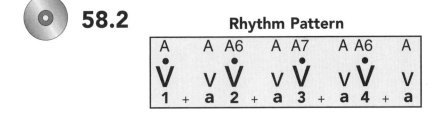

A		A	A6	A		A	A7	A	A6	A
V̇	v	V̇	v	V̇	v	V̇	v	V̇	v	V
1	+	a	2	+	a	3	+	a	4	+	a

* Although the 6th string is not played, for ease of changing from root 6 to root 5 rock chords, the first finger remains barring both the 5th and 6th strings.

LESSON FORTY FOUR

TIME SIGNATURES - SIMPLE AND COMPOUND TIME

In Lesson 8 the time signature was defined, and examples of $\frac{3}{4}$ and $\frac{4}{4}$ time were given. These are both illustrations of what is called simple time.

Simple time occurs when the beat falls on undotted notes (quarter notes, half notes, eighth notes etc.) and thus every beat is divisible by two. In $\frac{4}{4}$ time the basic beat is a quarter note, which can be split into groups of two thus:

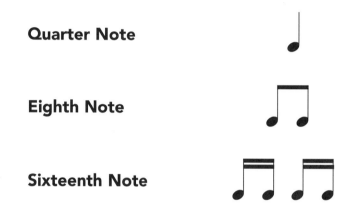

Quarter Note

Eighth Note

Sixteenth Note

Other common examples of simple time are $\frac{2}{4}$ and $\frac{3}{8}$. Two four time indicates 2 quarter note beats per bar, and three eight time indicates 3 eighth note beats per bar (rhythmically similar to three four time).

A beat can also occur on a dotted note, (revise Lesson 7), making it divisible into groups of 3. This is called **compound time.**

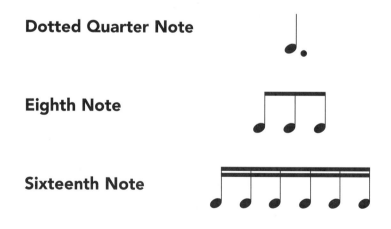

Dotted Quarter Note

Eighth Note

Sixteenth Note

The most common examples of compound time are $\frac{6}{8}$ and $\frac{12}{8}$. The interpretation of these time signatures is different from those of simple time. $\frac{6}{8}$ does not represent 6 eight note beats per bar. Instead it represents 2 dotted quarter note beats per bar. This is calculated by dividing the top number by 3, to get the number of beats per bar; and dividing the bottom number by 2 to get the type of dotted note receiving one beat. This results in a different rhythm feel for compound time. Compare $\frac{6}{8}$ to $\frac{3}{4}$ time, where they both can contain 6 eighth notes in a bar:

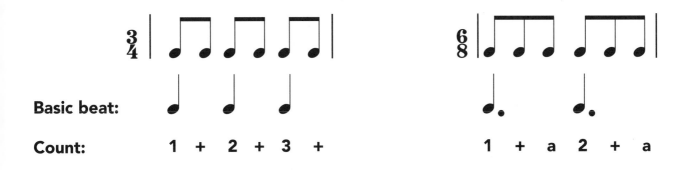

EXAMPLES IN $\frac{6}{8}$ TIME

In this turnaround, count in groups of six and place emphasis on the '1' and '4' counts, (i.e., where the beat occurs). Use bar chords.

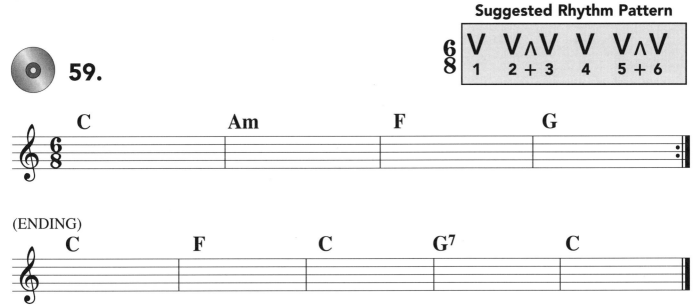

The ending used in this turnaround is a very common sequence of chords, following the pattern Ī - ĪV - Ī - V̄7 - Ī.

SECTION TWO SUMMARY

In Section Two you have covered the chords, rhythms and techniques used by most rhythm guitarists. If your ambition is to join a group, now is the time to do so. The only way to become a good rhythm guitarist is to **be** a rhythm guitarist in a group. The experience of being in a group will improve your playing immensely.

As well as being in a group, you need to listen to and copy other rhythm guitarists. Try to see as many 'live' groups as possible.

Written below is a summary of what has been covered in Section Two.

CHORDS: Root 6 bar chords: major, minor, dominant 7th, m7th, 6th.
Root 5 bar chords: major, minor, dominant 7th, m7th, 6th.
'Rock' chords.

RHYTHMS: Reggae
Triplet rhythm variation

TECHNIQUES: Percussive strum (L/H deadening technique
R/H deadening technique
Staccato strumming
Arpeggio picking
Dampening technique

THEORY: Key signatures
Major scales: C, G, D, A, E, F, B flat and E flat
Rests in music
Basic patterns: Blues and Turnarounds
Chord constructions: major, minor, dominant 7th, m7th, 6th
Time signatures: simple and compound time

Also read Appendices Four and Five; and revise Section One.

EXTRA PROGRESSIONS
PROGRESSIVE 1 - 'RAGTIME BLUES'

60. Use open chords, except for the A♭7 in bar 12

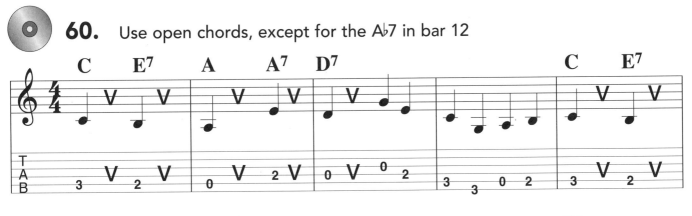

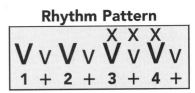

Rhythm Pattern

PROGRESSIVE 2 - 'ROCK BLUES'

61. Use 2 strings rock chords (root 6 and root 5) for the entire progression.

PROGRESSIVE 2 - 'CHORD MODULATION'

The following chord progression is based upon the chord sequence $\bar{I}$ - $\overline{III}7$ - $\overline{VI}m$ - $\bar{I}7$ modulatng through the keys of C, F, B♭, E♭, A♭, D♭, G♭, B, E, A, D, and G.

62.

SECTION THREE

LESSON FORTY FIVE

BAR CHORD FORMATIONS

The two bar chord shapes you have studied so far, root 6 (E formation) and root 5 (A formation), involves sliding an open chord along the fretboard, i.e. E open and A open respectively. This concept could be applied to all open chords, but due to awkward fingerings only a few shapes are practical.

One of the most useful chords to slide up the guitar is C major. Hold an open C chord, using the 2nd, 3rd and 4th fingers as illustrated below.

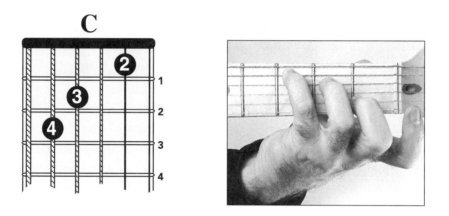

Now slide this shape up one fret, and bar with the first finger thus:

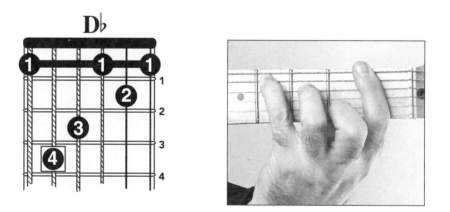

This chord shape has its root note on the 5th and 2nd strings, and shall be referred to as a 'C formation' bar chord. As with the other bar chords, it can be moved along the fretboard, changing name with each new position.

Try the following exercise, using the C formation bar chord in conjunction with root 6 and root 5 bar chords.

63.

```
┌─────────────────┐
│ V v v V v v      │
│ 1 + a 2 + a      │
└─────────────────┘
```

D♭ (1ST FRET)   B♭m (1ST FRET)   G♭ (2ND FRET)   A♭ (4TH FRET)

𝄞 2/4

'C FORMATION'   'A FORMATION'   'E FORMATION'   'E FORMATION'

E (4TH FRET)   C♯m (4TH FRET)   A (5TH FRET)   B (7TH FRET)

'C FORMATION'   'A FORMATION'   'E FORMATION'   'E FORMATION'

G (7TH FRET)   Em (7TH FRET)   C (8TH FRET)   D (10TH FRET)   G (7TH FRET)

'C FORMATION'   'A FORMATION'   'E FORMATION'   'E FORMATION'   'C FORMATION'

Note that the C formation bar chord is extremely useful in a major to relative minor chord progression.

LESSON FORTY SIX

SUSPENDED CHORDS

In Lesson 11 you were introduced to open suspended chords. The formula for a suspended chord is $\bar{1}$ - $\overline{IV}$ - $\bar{V}$. In most cases the suspended chord will resolve (lead back) to a major chord of the same name.

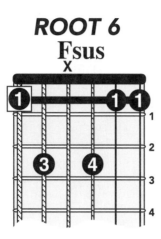

ROOT 6

Fsus

ROOT 5

B♭sus

The 4th string is deadened
with the third finger.

SUSPENDED EXAMPLE

In the following progression the chord change occurs before the first beat of the bar (on the second half of the fourth beat). Continuous right hand movement must be maintained throughout. Finish the last bar with a single strum.

64.

Rhythm Pattern

(ROOT 6)		(ROOT 5)		(ROOT 6)		(ROOT 5)
A	Asus	D	Dsus	G	Gsus	C

	(ROOT 6)		(ROOT 5)		(ROOT 6)	
Csus	F	Fsus	B♭	B♭sus	F	

* A very similar sounding chord is the 7sus, which contains the notes $\bar{1}$ - $\overline{IV}$ - $\bar{V}$ - $♭\overline{VII}$

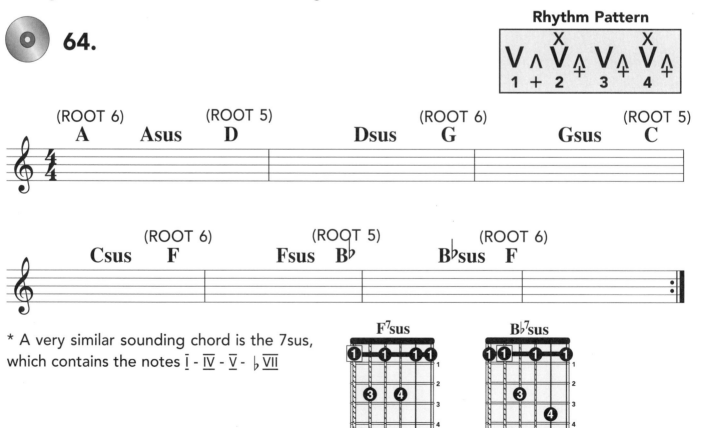

F⁷sus

B♭⁷sus

LESSON FORTY SEVEN

MAJOR SEVENTH CHORDS

ROOT 6

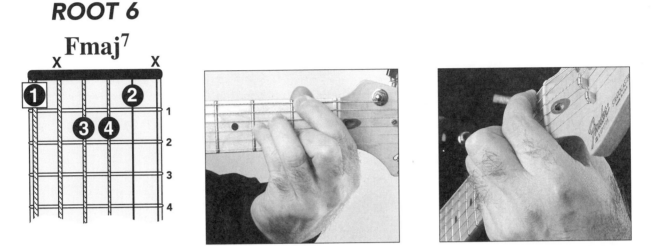

Fmaj⁷

Major 7th chords consist of the $\underline{\mathrm{I}}$ - $\underline{\mathrm{III}}$ - $\underline{\mathrm{V}}$ - $\underline{\mathrm{VII}}$ notes of the major scale. Thus Fmaj7 will contain the notes F A C E. The root 6 major 7 chords cannot be regarded as a bar chord, since the first finger is not barring all strings. You will notice from the photos that the first finger is actually curved, so that it plays the 6th string, and deadens the 5th and 1st strings.

65.

Rhythm Pattern

V̌	V̌	V̌	V̌
1	2	3	4

Gmaj⁷   Cmaj⁷   Gmaj⁷   Cmaj⁷

ROOT 5

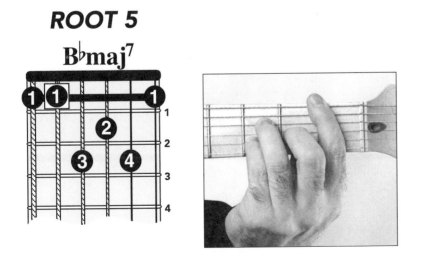

B♭maj⁷

This root 5 major 7th shape is derived from the open Amaj7 chord. Try the following example, using a combination of root 6 and root 5 major 7th chords:

66.

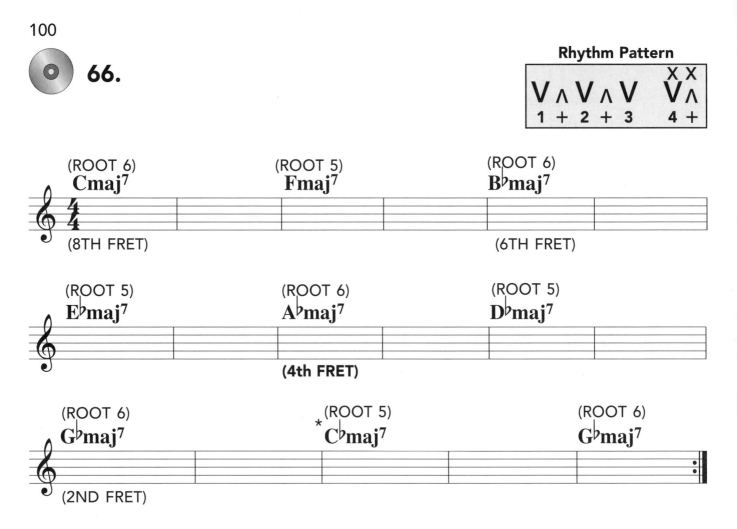

The basic progression used in this example example involves a pattern of fourths; i.e. Fmaj7 is a fourth higher than C, B♭maj7 is a fourth higher than F and so on:

Cmaj7 - Fmaj7 - B♭maj7 - E♭maj 7 - A♭maj7 - D♭maj7 - G♭maj7 - C♭maj7

This concept of progressing in fourths is particularly common with major 7th chords.

* This is the same as Bmaj7.

LESSON FORTY EIGHT

OFF BEAT RHYTHMS

Most rhythms studied so far have had the emphasis placed on the 'on' beat (1...2...3...4...). However, many interesting rhythms can be created by deadening the 'on' beat, and strumming on the 'off' beat, as illustrated in this example:

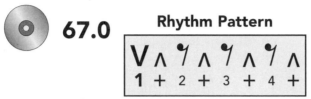

67.0

In this rhythm pattern the eighth note rest occurs **on** the beat, and is created by using the right hand deadening technique. Apply this rhythm to the following progression (use open or bar chords).

67.1

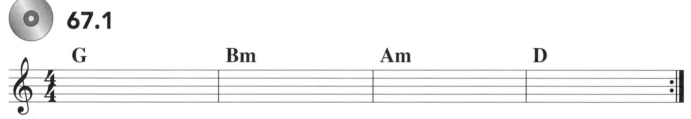

Experimentation is the best way to discover new off-beat rhythms. Try the following variations:

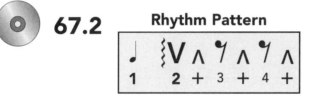

67.2

Play this off-beat rhythm against the following progression (use open or bar chords).

67.3

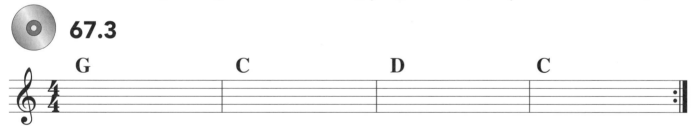

The following 2 bar rhythm is referred to as a 'Bossa Nova.'

68.0

68.1

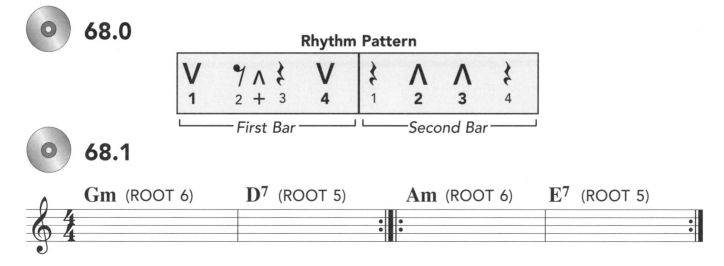

LESSON FORTY NINE

NINTH CHORDS

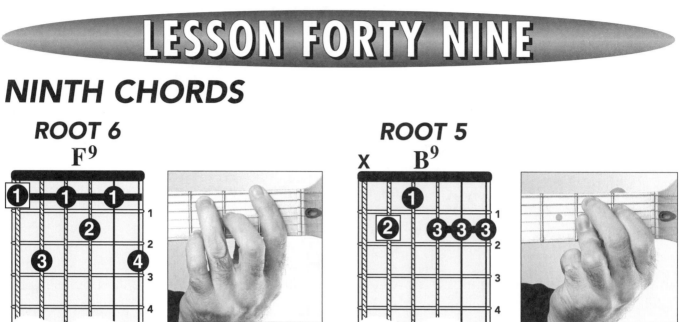

ROOT 6 — F⁹

ROOT 5 — X B⁹

When playing the root 5 ninth chord, the third finger forms a half bar across the first three strings. For ease of playing the third finger is positioned first. The thumb or the tip of the 2nd finger can be used to deaden the sixth string.

The ninth chord consists of the $\underline{I}$ - $\underline{III}$ - $\underline{V}$ - $\flat\underline{VII}$ - $\underline{IX}$ notes of the major scale. It can be thought of as an extension of the dominant seventh chord, with the ninth note added (in terms of the major scale, the ninth note is the same as the second:

	$\underline{I}$	$\underline{III}$	$\underline{V}$	$\flat\underline{VII}$	$\underline{IX}$
F9:	F	A	C	E♭	G
C9:	C	E	G	B♭	D

CHORD SUBSTITUTION

Chord substitution involves playing a different set of chords for a given chord progression. In the two following examples, the chord substitutions used are:

> major7 for major
> major6 for major
> minor7 for minor
> ninth for dominant 7th

* An alternative fingering for the root 5 ninth chord involves deadening the fifth string and playing the sixth string, as such:

* In this form the root note is omitted. For chords consisting of 5 or more notes it is permissible to omit the 1st and/or the 5th note of that chord. Omitting these notes does not alter the characteristic sound of the chord.

X B⁹

TURNAROUND IN A

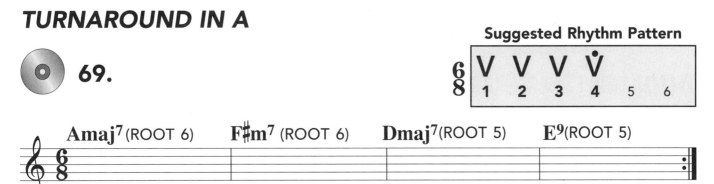

69.

This type of substitution gives a jazz sound.

JAZZ BLUES IN B♭

70.

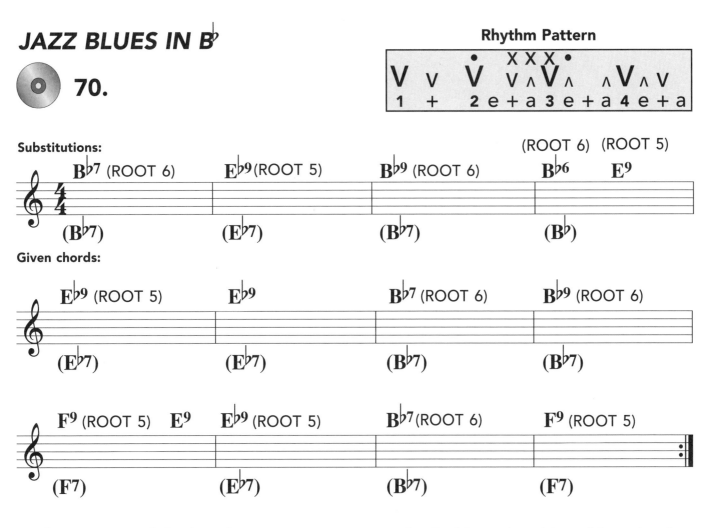

In this suggested rhythm the staccato strum on the 2nd beat is achieved by releasing pressure with the left hand. In bar 9th, the passing chord principle, as outlined in Lesson 14 is used. The substitution that you have been using can be applied to the chord progression on page 94.

The substitution that you have been using can be applied to the chord progression on page 94.

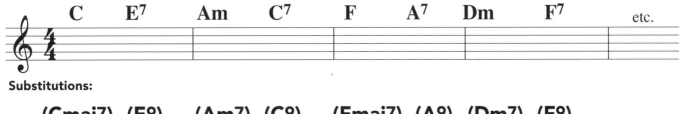

LESSON FIFTY

AUGMENTED CHORDS

F+, A+, D♭+,

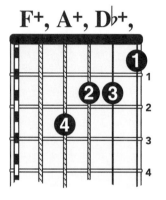

The **+** symbol is used to indicate an augmented chord. Sometimes the abbreviation 'Aug' is used.

This augmented chord shape actually has three different names. To understand why this is so, examine the formula for an augmented chord: $\underline{I}$ - $\underline{III}$ - $\sharp\underline{V}$. By applying this formula to their respective scales, it can be seen that F+, A+ and D♭+ all contain the same notes, thus the same shape can be used for all three chords.

	$\underline{I}$	$\underline{III}$	$\sharp\underline{V}$
F+	F	A	C♯
A+	A	C♯	E♯(F)
D♭+	D♭	F	A

(D♭+ can also be called C♯+)

Because each shape represents three different chords, the complete range of augmented chords is covered by using the shape over four frets. At the first fret it is either F+, A+ or D♭+; at the second it is F♯+, B♭+ or D+; at the third it is G+, B+, or E♭+; and at the fourth it is A♭+, C+ or E+. This covers all the possible augmented chords, and when you reach the fifth fret the shape will be F+, A+ or D♭+ again (as at the first fret).

The easiest way to remember the three different augmented names involved in each shape is simply to read off the notes contained when that shape is held; i.e. if the augmented shape is played at the third position, and the individual notes are named (G, B, E♭, G) this gives the three names of the augmented chord (G+, B+, and E♭+). Conversely, if you wish to play a given augmented chord (C+), all you need to do is find a C note on any of the four strings, and then play the augmented shape around it (the shape you play will also produce an A♭+ or E+). A C note can be found on the third string at the fifth fret, so the chord will be formed thus:

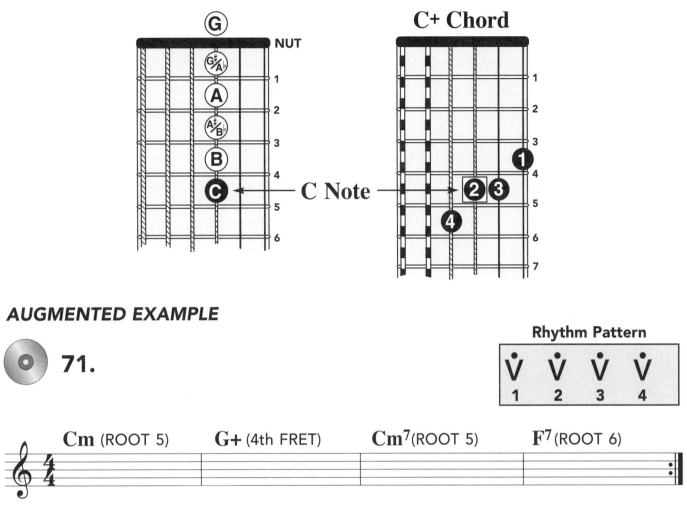

G

C+ Chord

C Note

AUGMENTED EXAMPLE

71.

Rhythm Pattern

Ꜣ	Ꜣ	Ꜣ	Ꜣ
1	2	3	4

Cm (ROOT 5)   **G+** (4th FRET)   **Cm⁷**(ROOT 5)   **F⁷** (ROOT 6)

The G+ used in this example can be played at the third fret (G note located on both the first and fourth strings). Since both the Cm and Cm7 chords involve barring with the first finger, you will find it easier to change chords if the bar is held through the G+ chord. When you do this, be sure only to play the first four strings.

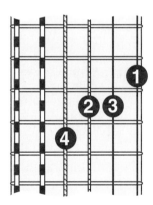

Do NOT play the fifth and sixth strings.

Using the first four strings only for the augmented chord results in a strong treble sound. Another way of playing it is to replace the first string note with the equivalent sixth string note:

"TREBLE" SOUND

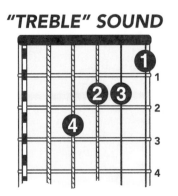

"BASS" SOUND

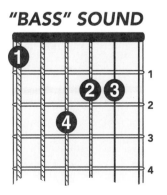

The bass form may be preferred in some instances, especially when bass note picking is involved.

LESSON FIFTY ONE

DIMINISHED CHORDS

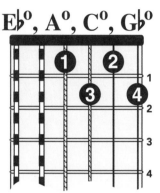

$E\flat^0, A^0, C^0, G\flat^0$

Apart from the ^{0}, other symbols used for a diminished chord are the abbreviation 'dim,' or a minus sign; e.g. 'Cdim' or C-' represent C^0.

Each diminished shape represents four different diminished chords. The formula for a diminished chord is $\underline{I}$ - $\flat\underline{III}$ - $\flat\underline{V}$ - $\flat\flat\underline{VII}$ *, so an analysis of the given shape reveals:

$E\flat^0$ can also be called $D\sharp^0$
$G\flat^0$ can also be called $F\sharp^0$

	$\underline{I}$	$\flat\underline{III}$	$\flat\underline{V}$	$\flat\underline{VII}$
$E\flat^0$	$E\flat$	$G\flat$	$B\flat\flat(A)$	$D\flat\flat (C)$
A^0	A	C	$E\flat$	$G\flat$
C^0	C	$E\flat$	$G\flat$	$B\flat\flat (A)$
$G\flat^0$	G	$B\flat\flat (A)$	$D\flat\flat (C)$	$F\flat\flat (E\flat)$

Because each shape represents four diminished chords, the complete range is covered in three frets and thus each shape repeats the same chords every three frets. Try playing the shape above at the first fret, then the fourth, seventh and tenth frets. You are playing the same chord each time but the movement up the guitar neck creates an interesting and suspenseful sound.

72.

Rhythm Pattern

V		V	∧	V	∧	V	∧
1		2	+	3	+	4	+

$E\flat$**dim** (1ST POS.)　　(4TH POS.)　　　　(7TH POS.)　　　　(10TH POS.)

$\frac{4}{4}$

73. Try the following example, using a $B\flat^0$ at the second position, and open shapes for the other chords.

Rhythm Pattern

V		V	∧	V	∧
1		2	+	3	+

G　　　　　$B\flat$**dim**　　　　Am　　　　D^7

$\frac{3}{4}$

Although only one shape is necessary for diminished chords, there are two others that are frequently used by guitarists:

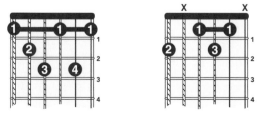

* A double flat sign ($\flat\flat$) lowers the note's pitch by one tone (two semitones). For double sharps a cross (**x**) is used, e.g. C**x** = D

LESSON FIFTY TWO

ROOT 6 SIXTH CHORDS - ALTERNATIVE FORM

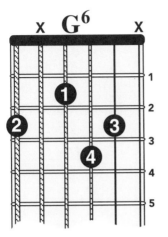

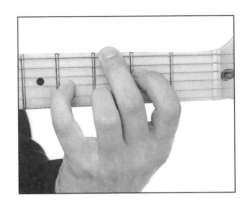

This sixth chord shape is frequently used in progressions which require a 'jazz' flavour. It is often used in conjunction with the major and major 7th chords, as illustrated below:

74.

Rhythm Pattern

V	V̇	V	V̇
1	2	3	4

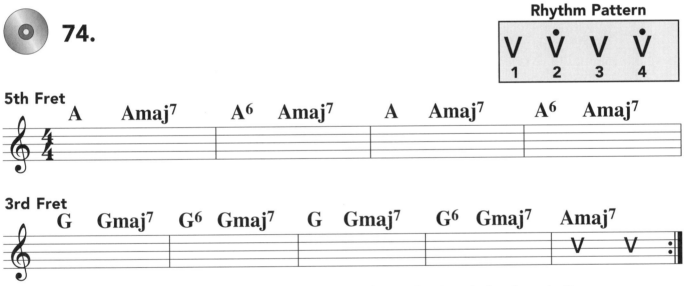

5th Fret
A   Amaj⁷   A⁶   Amaj⁷   A   Amaj⁷   A⁶   Amaj⁷

3rd Fret
G   Gmaj⁷   G⁶   Gmaj⁷   G   Gmaj⁷   G⁶   Gmaj⁷   Amaj⁷

When changing from the major 7th chord to the sixth chord the fourth finger acts as a pivot, remaining in position on the third string. Chord changing will be much easier if this principle is applied.

ROOT 6 MINOR 7TH CHORD - ALTERNATIVE FORM

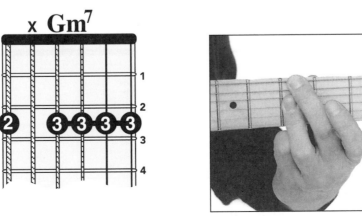

With the minor 7th chord shown on the previous page, and other jazz flavoured chords studied so far (i.e. 9th, 6th and maj7 chords) the wrist moves into a different position, as illustrated in the photos:

Wrist position for bar chords:

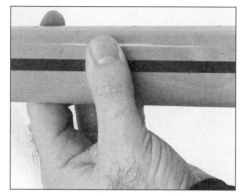

Wrist position for jazz chords:

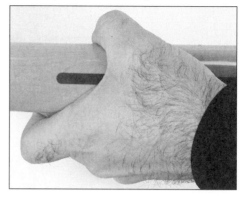

Play the following example, using the alternative fingering for the m7th chords:

75.

Rhythm Pattern

V ∧ V ∧ V̇ V̇
1 + 2 + 3   4

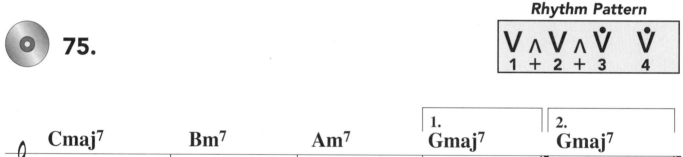

| Cmaj⁷ | Bm⁷ | Am⁷ | 1. Gmaj⁷ | 2. Gmaj⁷ |

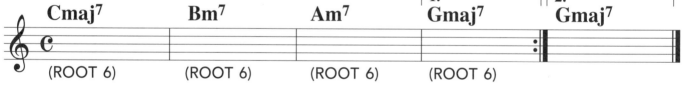

(ROOT 6)   (ROOT 6)   (ROOT 6)   (ROOT 6)

ROOT 6 MINOR 6TH CHORD

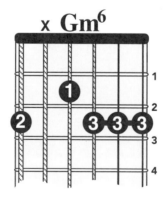

x Gm⁶

The formula for a m6th chord is $\underline{I}$ - $\flat\underline{III}$ - $\underline{V}$ - $\underline{VI}$. From this, it can be seen that the m6th is an extension of the minor chord, adding the 6th note of the scale:

	$\underline{I}$	$\flat\underline{III}$	$\underline{V}$	$\underline{VI}$
Gm6:	G	B♭	D	E
Cm6:	C	E♭	G	A

* This minor 6th chord shape is the same as the alternative given for the 9th chord in Lesson 49.

JAZZ BLUES IN G

This example combines all root 6 jazz flavoured chords so far studied in this lesson. Experiment with different rhythms and bass note picking.

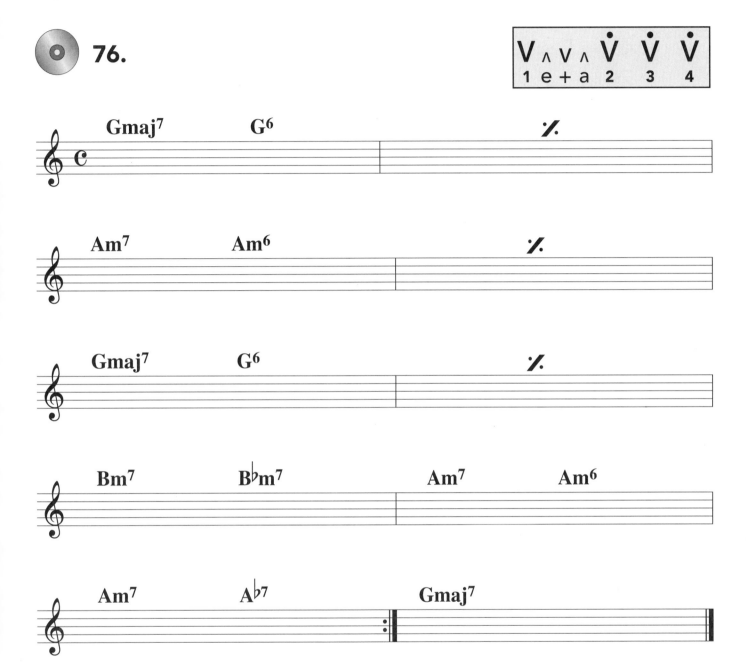

LESSON FIFTY THREE

DOMINANT 7TH CHORD - ALTERNATIVE FORM

In Lesson 7 you were introduced to the open C7 chord thus:

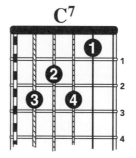

This can be converted into a moveable chord shape by repositioning the third finger onto the sixth string, and deadening the fifth and first strings.

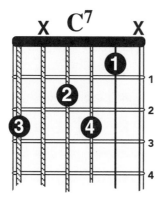

The first finger deadens the first string, and the third finger deadens the fifth string.

The re-location of the third finger does not change the chord name because it still contains the correct notes;

	$\bar{\text{I}}$	$\overline{\text{III}}$	$\bar{\text{V}}$	$\flat\overline{\text{VII}}$
i.e.	C	E	G	B$\flat$

By following the chromatic scale (starting on C) this chord shape can be played at any position on the fretboard.

e.g. 1st fret - C7   3rd fret - D7   6th fret - F7 etc.

77.

Rhythm Pattern

V	V	V	V
1	2	3	4

F F⁷ B♭ B♭m   F C⁷ F C♯⁷ F♯ F♯⁷ B Bm   F♯ C♯⁷ F♯ D⁷

G G⁷ C Cm   G D⁷ G E♭⁷ A♭ A♭⁷ D♭ D♭m   A♭ E♭⁷ A♭ E⁷ etc.

This example follows a set pattern (over 2 bars) which moves up the fretboard one semitone at a time.

12 BAR IN D

The following 12 bar blues uses the moveable 7th chord shape studied in this lesson.

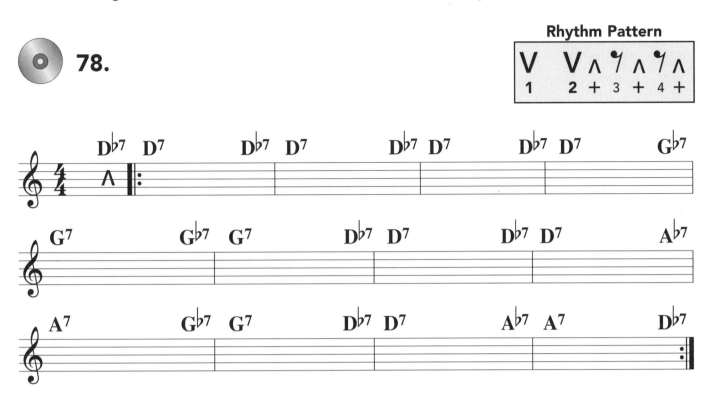

This progression begins on the 'and' strum of the fourth beat, before the first bar. This is called a lead in or anacrusis (i.e. beginning before the first beat).

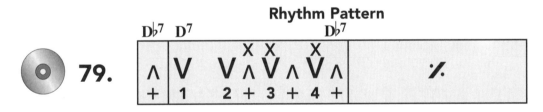

Try this alternative rhythm using percussive strums as indicated. To achieve the correct sound, release pressure on the chord shape.

A variation to this rhythm involves the use of a slide technique on the 1st beat. This is achieved by sliding the chord shape up 1 fret, without releasing pressure. Do not strum on the 1st beat, indicated thus:

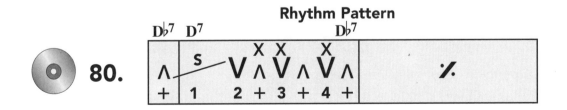

LESSON FIFTY FOUR

SIXTEENTH NOTE RHYTHM

81.0

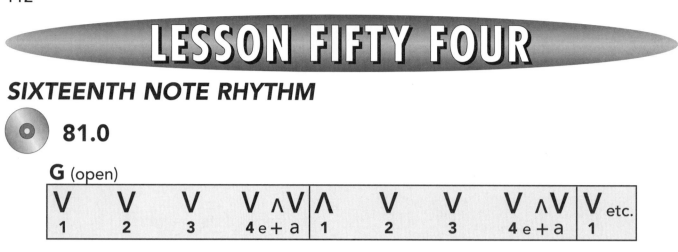

G (open)

V	V	V	V ∧ V	∧	V	V	V ∧ V	V etc.
1	2	3	4 e + a	1	2	3	4 e + a	1

The above rhythm uses an up stroke on the first beat of every bar (except for the first bar). Play the following turnaround, using the new rhythm and open chords.

81.1

∧	V	V	V ∧ V
1	2	3	4 e + a

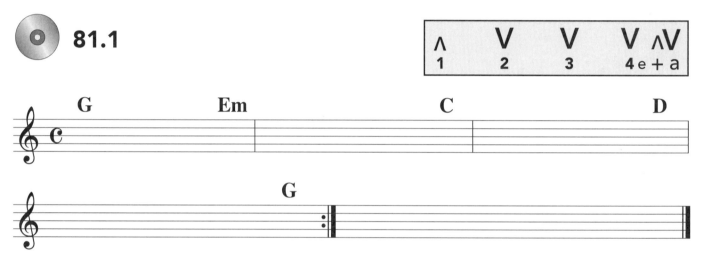

You will notice that the chord change occurs on the second half of the fourth beat (i.e. 'and a').

SIXTEENTH NOTE RHYTHM VARIATIONS

This sixteenth note rhythm (4 strums in one beat) can be varied to obtain many different patterns.

Three variations are listed below:

82.0   **Am7** (ROOT 6)

V	V	∧ V	V	V	X V
1	2 e + a	3	+	4	+

Apply this rhythm to the following progression:

82.1

Am⁷ (ROOT 6)   F♯m⁷ (ROOT 6)   Am⁷   F♯m⁷

Example 82.1 can be made more interesting if you add bass note picking and percussive strumming. Play the sixth string bass note on the first beat of the bar.

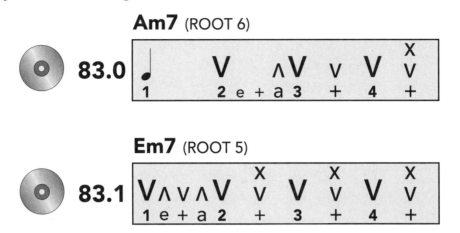

Apply the rhythm in example 83.1 to the following chord progression:

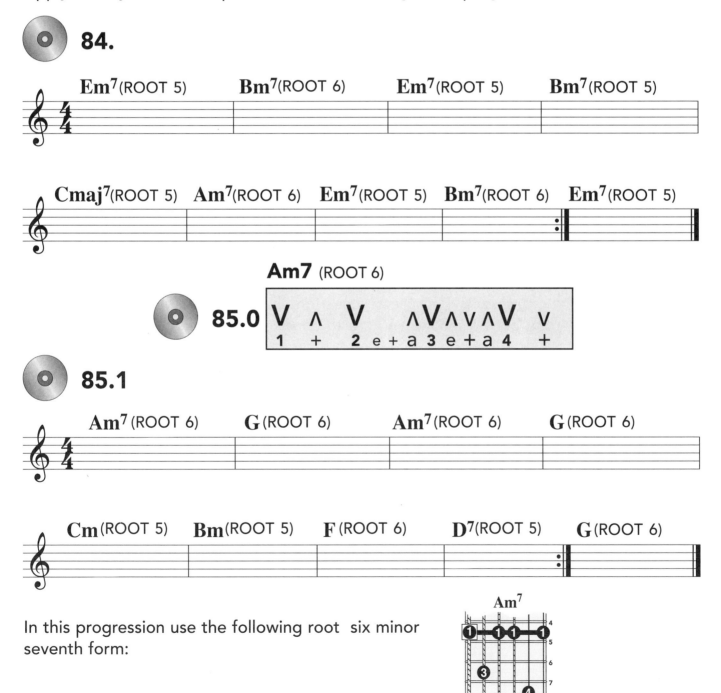

In this progression use the following root six minor seventh form:

SECTION THREE SUMMARY

In Section Three you have studied the more advanced aspects of rhythm guitar playing. It is essential for you now to adapt the material you have studied to the type of music you wish to play (in either group or solo performance). To do this you will need to listen carefully and experiment with everything you are playing.

Here is a summary of what has been covered in Section Three.

CHORDS: Alternative bar chord formations: C formation chords
Root 6 bar chords: sus, sus7, maj7, 9th, m6
Root 5 bar chords: sus, sus7, maj7, 9th, m6
Augmented and diminished chords
Alternative chord forms: 6th, m7, 7th

RHYTHMS: Off beat rhythms
Sixteenth note rhythm variations.

THEORY: Chord constructions: sus, sus7, maj7, 9th, aug, dim, m6

Revise Sections One and Two. Re-read all Appendices. Read Glossary of Musical Terms, Chord Formula Chart, etc.

EXTRA PROGRESSIONS

86   **Progression 1.** Be sure to use right hand deadening for the staccato strums on the second and fourth beats.

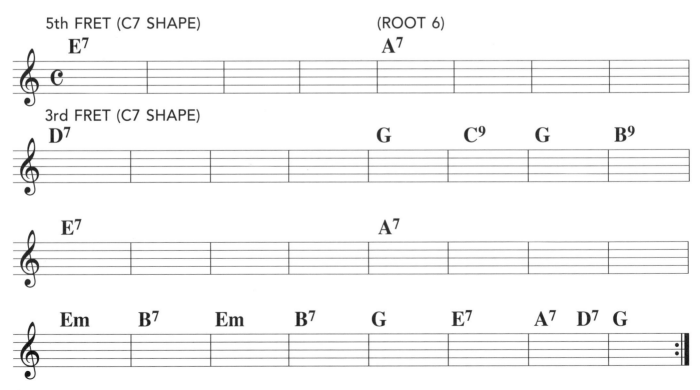

87 **Progression 2.** Use jazz chord shapes for the G6 and Am7 chords (Lesson 52) in this progression, and use the G♯dim chord with the root note (G♯) in the bass. Experiment with bass note picking and rhythm patterns (Lesson 54).

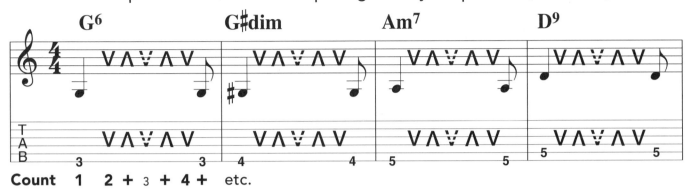

Count 1 2 + 3 + 4 + etc.

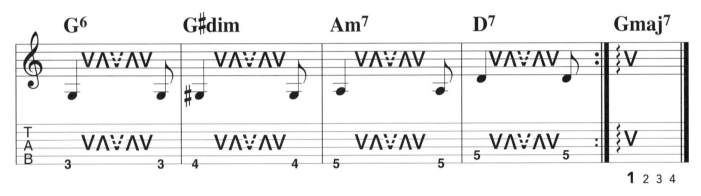

88

Progression 3. The Bm9 and F♯7+ chords used in this progression are illustrated below (in root 6 form).

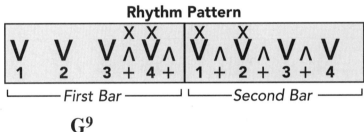

Rhythm Pattern

├── First Bar ──┤ ├── Second Bar ──┤

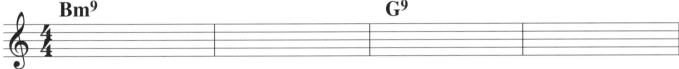

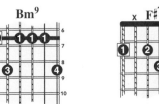

Progression 4. This progression follows the pattern of fourths (see Lesson 47) every four bars. Use root 6 and root 5 bar chord shapes (no alternative form chords).

89.

Rhythm Pattern

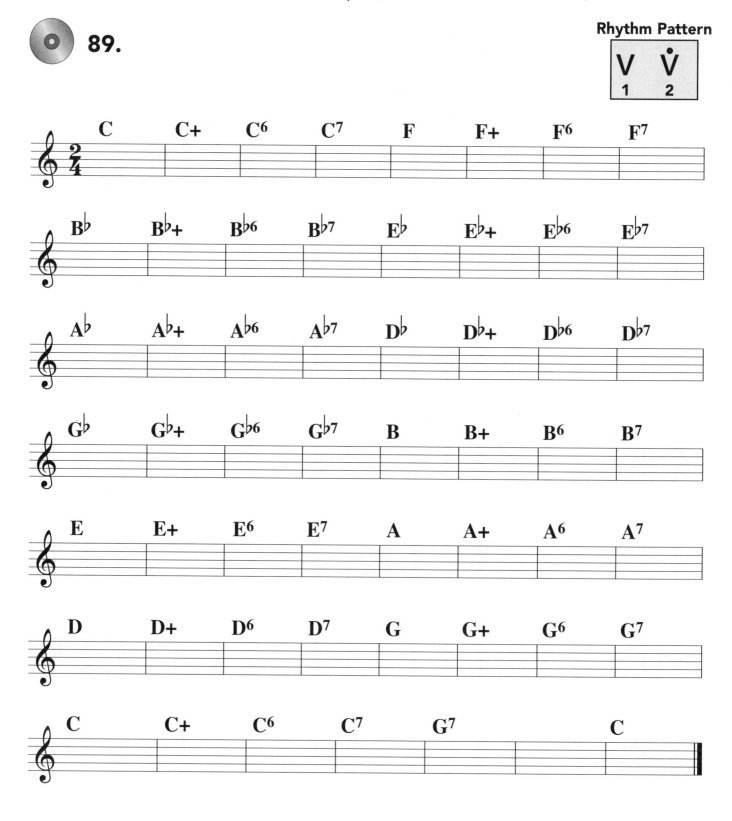

Progression 5. Use root 6 and root 5 jazz flavoured chords in this progression.

90.

Rhythm Pattern

V V V V
1 2 3 4

Em⁷	A⁷	Dmaj⁷	F♯m⁷ Fm⁷ Em⁷	A¹³
(ROOT 5)	(ROOT 6)	(ROOT 5)	(ROOT 5)	(ROOT 6)

Em^7 (ROOT 5) A^7 (ROOT 6) $Dmaj^7$ (ROOT 5) $F\#m^7$ Fm^7 Em^7 (ROOT 5) A^{13} (ROOT 6)

$Dmaj^7$ (ROOT 5) Bm^7 Am^7 $A\flat m^7$ (ROOT 6) $D\flat 9$ (ROOT 5) $G\flat maj^7$ (ROOT 6) $G\flat 6$ (ROOT 6)

$A\flat m^7$ (ROOT 6) $D\flat 9$ (ROOT 5) $G\flat 6$ (ROOT 6) $B\flat m^7$ Bm^7 Cm^7 (ROOT 6) F^{13} (ROOT 5)

Dm^9 (ROOT 5) Gm^9 (ROOT 6) Em^9 (ROOT 5) A^{13} (ROOT 6) $Dmaj^7$ (ROOT 5) V

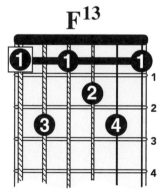

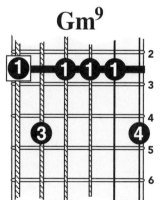

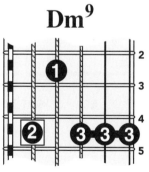

The A13 chord uses this shape at the 5th fret.

The Em9 chord uses this shape at the 5th fret.

APPENDIX ONE - TUNING

It is essential for your guitar to be in tune, so that the chords and notes you play will sound correct. The main problem with tuning for most beginning students is that the ear is not able to determine slight differences in pitch. For this reason you should seek the aid of a teacher or an experienced guitarists.

Several methods can be used to tune the guitar. These include:

1. Tuning to another musical instrument (e.g. piano, guitar or another guitar).
2. Tuning to pitch pipes or a tuning fork
3. Tuning the guitar to itself.
4. Using an electronic tuner.

The most common and useful of these is tuning the guitar to itself. This method involves finding notes of the same pitch on different strings. The adjacent diagram outlines the notes used:

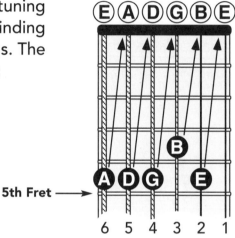

The method of tuning is as follows:

1. Tune the open sixth string to either:
   (a) The open sixth string of another guitar.
   (b) A piano.

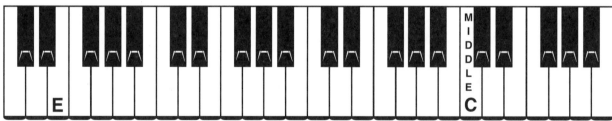

The piano key equivalent to the open 6th string is indicated on the diagram above.

(c) Pitch pipes, which produce notes that correspond with each of the 6 open strings.

(d) A tuning fork. Most tuning forks give the note A.

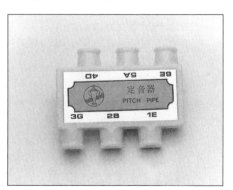

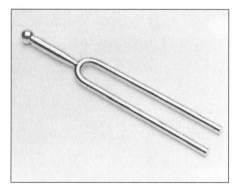

To produce sound from the tuning fork, hold it by the stem and tap one of the prongs against something hard. This will set up a vibration, which can be heard clearly when the bass of the stem is then placed on a solid surface, e.g. a guitar body.

2.   Place a finger on the 6th string at the fifth fret. Now play the open A (5th string). If the guitar is to be in tune, then these two notes must have the same pitch (i.e. sound the same). If they do not sound the same, the 5th string must be adjusted to match the note produced on the 6th string, i.e. it is tuned in relation to the 6th string.

3.   Tune the open 4th string to the note on the fifth fret of the 5th string, using the method outlined above.

4.   Tune all other strings using the same procedure, remembering that the open B string (2nd) is tuned to the 4th fret (check diagram) while all other strings are tuned to the 5th fret.

5.   Strum an open E major chord, to check if your guitar is tuned correctly. At first may have some difficulty deciding whether or not the chord sound is correct, but as your ear improves you will become more familiar with the correct sound of the chord.

Tuning may take you many months to master, and you should practice it constantly. The guidance of a teacher will be an invaluable aid in the early stages of guitar tuning.

TUNING HINTS

One of the easiest ways to practice tuning is to actually start with the guitar in tune and then de-tune one string. When you do this, always take the string **down** in pitch (i.e. loosen it) as it is easier to tune "up" to a given note rather than "down" to it. As an example, de-tune the 4th string (D). If you strum a chord now, the guitar will sound out of tune, even though only one string has been altered (so remember that if your guitar is out of tune it may only be one string at fault.)

Following the correct method, you must tune the 4th string against the D note at the fifth fret of the 5th string. Play the note loudly, and listen carefully to the sound produced. This will help you retain the correct pitch in your mind when tuning the next string.

Now that you have listened carefully to the note that you want, the D string must be tuned to it. Play the D string, and turn its tuning key at the same time, and you will hear the pitch of the string change (it will become higher as the tuning key tightens the string). It is important to follow this procedure, so that you hear the sound of the string at all times, as it tightens. You should also constantly refer back to the correct sound that is required (i.e. the D note on the fifth fret of the 5th string).

ELECTRONIC TUNERS

Electronic tuners make tuning your guitar very easy. They allow you to tune each string individually to the tuner, by indicating whether the notes are sharp (too high) or flat (too low). It is still recommended however, that you practice tuning your guitar by the above method to help improve your musicianship.

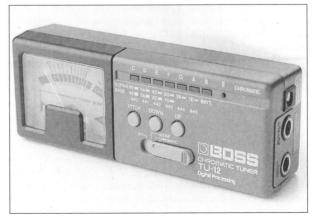

Electronic Tuner

APPENDIX TWO - SONG LIST

In the first section of this book two basic chord progressions are introduced; 12 bar blues and turnarounds (1 and 2). These two progressions are the basis of many songs from the fifties onwards, some of which are listed below.

12 BAR BLUES

Be-bop-a-lula – Gene Vincent/John Lennon
Hound Dog – Elvis Presley
Johnny B. Goode – Chuck Berry
Boppin' the Blues – Blackfeather
The Wanderer – Dion
Going up the Country – Canned Heat
Makin' Your Mind Up – Bucks Fizz
Green Door – Shakin' Stevens
In the Summertime – Mungo Jerry
Rock Around the Clock – Bill Haley & The Commets
Barbara Ann – The Beach Boys
Let's Stick Together – Bryan Ferry
Long Tall Glasses (I Know I Can Dance) – Leo Sayer
Blue Suede Shoes – Elvis Presley
School Days (Ring Ring Goes the Bell) – Chuck Berry
Roll Over Beethoven – Chuck Berry
Spirit in the Sky – Norman Greenbaum
Turn Up Your Radio – The Masters Apprentices
Tutti Frutti – Little Richard
Dizzy Miss Lizzy – larry Williams/The Beatles
Peggy Sue – Buddy Holly
Jailhouse Rock – Elvis Presley
Get Down and Get With It – Slade
Good Golly Miss Molly – Little Richard
Lucille – Little Richard

In the Mood – Glen Miller
Surfin' Safari – The Beach Boys
Peppermint Twist – Sweet
Boogie Woogie Bugle Boy – The Andrew Sisters/Bett Midler
I Hear You Knocking – Dave Edmunds
Boy From New York City – Darts/Manhattan Transfer
Mountain of Love – Johnny Rivers
I Love to Boogie – T-Rex
Shake Rattle & Roll – Bill Hayley
Lady Rose – Mungo Jerry
Theme to Batman
Theme to Spiderman
Stuck in the Middle with you – Stealers Wheel
Hot Love – T-Rex
The Huckle Buck – Brendan Bower
Way Down – Elvis Presley
I Can Help – Billy Swan
Rockin' Robin – Michael Jackson
Red House – Jimi Hendrix
Texas Flood – Stevie Ray Vaughan
Killing Floor – Jimi Hendrix
The Jack – ACDC
Ice Cream Man - Van Halen
Oh Pretty Woman – Gary Moore

TURNAROUND ONE *

I Will Always Love You – Whitney Houston
The Night Has a 1000 Eyes – Bobby Vee
It's Raining Again – Supertramp
More – Various Artists
Ti Amo – Umberto Tozzi
Crocodile Rock (chorus) – Elton John
One Last Kiss – Various Artists
Stand By Me – John Lennon
Dream – Everly Brothers
Return to Sender – Elvis Presley
Telstar – Tornadoes
Always Look on the Bright Side of Life – Monty Python
Why do Fools Fall in Love – Frankie Lyman/Diana Ross
Sarah – Fleetwood Mac
Take Good Care of my Baby – Bobby Vee/Smokey
Where have all the Flowers Gone – Various Artists
Turnaround Sue – Dion & the Belmonts
Tell Me Why – The Beatles
Let's Twist Again – Chubby Checker
Stay (Just a Little Bit Longer) – The Four Seasons/
    Jackson Brown
Cool for Cats – U.K. Squeeze
Y.M.C.A – The Village People
Tired of Toein' the Line – rock Burnett
You Drive Me Crazy – Shakin' Stevens
Should I do it – Pointer Sisters
Poor Little Fool – Rick Nelson
You Don't Have to Say You Love Me – Dusty
Springfield/Elvis Presley
Breaking up is Hard to do – Neil Sedaka/

Partridge Family
Oh Carol – Neil Sedaka
Two Faces Have I – Lou Christie
Every Day – Buddy Hoily
Poetry in Motion – Johnny Tillotson
Sweet Little 16 – Neil Sedaka
Big Girls Don't Cry – Four Seasons
Sherry – Four Seasons
How Do You Do It – Jerry & The Pacemakers
Shour, Shout – Rocky Sharp & The Replays
Aces With You – Moon martin
Houses of the Holy – Led Zeppelin
Uptown Girl – Billy Joel
Buils Me Up Buttercup – The Foundations
'Happy Days' – Theme
Joane – Michael Nesmith
Goodnight Sweetheart – Various Artists
Looking For An Echo – Ol'55
Summer Holiday – Cliff Richard
Be My Baby – The Ronettes/Rachel Sweet
Everlasting Love – Rachel Sweet/Love Affair
I Go To Pieces (verse) – Peter & Gordon
Love Hurts – Everly Brothers/Jim
Capaldi/Nazareth
Gee Baby – Peter Shelley
Classic – Adrian Gurvitz
Teenage Dream – T-Rex
Blue Moon – Various Artists
The Tide is High – Blondie
Dennis – Blondie
It Ain't Easy – Normie Rowe

My World – Bee Gees
Hey Paula – Various Artists
It's Only Make Believe – Glen Campbell
Can't Smile Without You – Barry Manilow
Take Good Care of My Baby – Bobby
Vee/Smokie
Crossfire – Bellamy Brothers
Bobby's Girl – Marcie Blane
Do That To Me One More Time – Captain & Tenile
Please Mr Postman – Carpenters/ The Beatles
Sharin' The Night Together – Dr Hook
9 to 5 (Morning Train) – Sheena Easton
Diana – Paul Anka
Enola Gay – Orchestral Manoeuvres in the Dark
Some Guys Have All the Luck – Robert Palmer
So Lonely – Get Wet
Hungry Heart – Bruce Springsteen
Land of Make Believe (chorus) – Buck Fizz
Daddys Home – Cliff Richard
The Wonder of You – Elvis Presley
So You Win Again – Hot Chocolate
Hang Five – Rolling Stones
Paper Tiger – Sue Thompson
Venus – Frankie Avalon
Costafine Town – Splinter
If You Leave – OMD
True Blue – Madonna

TURNAROUND TWO

Crocodile Rock (verse) – Elton John
I started a Joke – The Bee Gees
Different Drum – Linda Ronstadt
Key Largo – Bertie Giggins
Black Berry Way – The Move
Georgy Girl – Seekers
Where Do You Go To My Lovely – Peter Sarsted
Mrs Brown, You've Got a Lovely Daughter –
    Hermans Hermit
Toast and Marmalade for Tea – Tin Tin
Movie Star – Harpo

It's A Heatache – Bonnie Tyler
I Don't Like Mondays – The Boomtown Rats
My Angel Baby – Toby Beau
Land Of Make Believe (verse) – Bucks Fizz
I'm In the Mood for Dancing – The Nolans
What's in a Kiss – Gilbert O'Sullivan
My Baby Loves Love – Joe Jeffries
Dreamin' – Johnny Burnett
Cruel To Be Kind – Nick Lowe
Where Did Our Love Go – Diana Ross & The

Supremes
Hurdy Gurdy Man – Donovan
I Go To Pieces (chorus) – Peter & Gordon
Get It Over With – Angie Gold
Sad Sweet Dreamer – Sweet Sensation
Down Town – Petula Clark
Easy – Oakridge Boys
Only You Can Do It – Francoiose hardy
Costafine – Splinter (chorus)
Where Did Our Love Go? – Phil Collins

SHEET MUSIC

You should try to work from sheet music as much as possible. Nearly all sheet music is arranged for piano and this presents problems for guitarists. Piano music uses three staves thus:

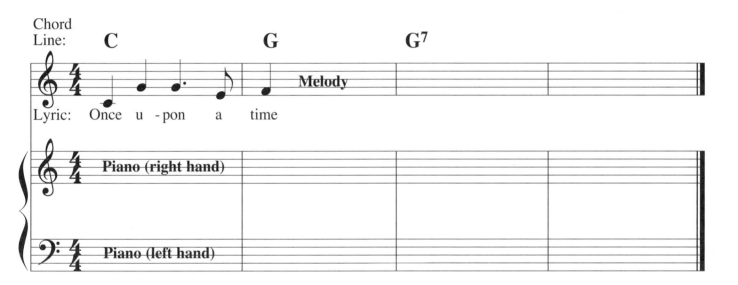

A guitar player need only look at the top stave, which contains the melody line (the tune), the lyrics and the chords. Sheet music does not indicate what rhythm the guitarist should use. This is where your creativity and background of rhythm playing (i.e. rhythms and techniques outlined in this book etc.) must be put to use. You should generally only attempt songs that you know well, and listen to original recordings of these songs to gain rhythm ideas.

APPENDIX THREE - TRANSPOSING

The term 'Transposing' is used to describe the process whereby a progressin (or song) is changed from one key to another. This is done for two main reasons:

1.   Singing - to sing the whole song at a lower or higher pitch (depending on the singer's vocal range).
2.   Ease of playing - because of the musical structure of the guitar, some keys are easier to play in than others. (e.g. Beginning students may not be able to play a song in the key of say E♭, but could perhaps play it in the key of C).

Consider the following turnaround in the key of C:

If you needed to transpose this progression into the key of G, the following method may be used:

1.   Write out the C chromatic* scale.
2.   Write out the G chromatic scale, with each note directly below its counterpart in the C chromatic scale, as such:

C chromatic   C   C♯ D   D♯ E   F   F♯ G   G♯ A   A♯ B   C
                  1↓   3↓   4↓   2↓

G chromatic   G   G♯ A   A♯ B   C   C♯ D   D♯ E   F   F♯ G

3.   When the given progression is transposed to the key of G, the first chord, C major, will become G major. This can be seen by relating the two chromatic scales via arrow one.
4.   The second chord of the progression, Am, will become Em (arrow 2). Although the name will change when transposing, its **type** (i.e. major, minor seventh etc.) will remain the same.
5.   The complete transposition will be:

Key of C:

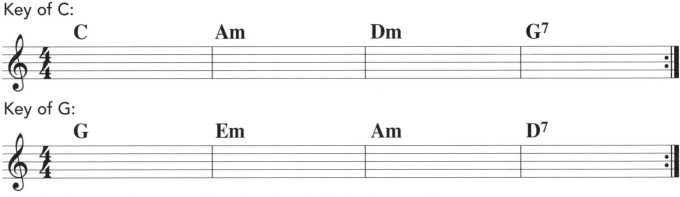

Key of G:

Play both progressions and notice the similarity in sound.

* See Glossary

In the early stages you will mainly transpose for ease of playing, and thus the easiest keys for a song to be transposed into are C, G and D (for major keys) and Am, Em and Bm (for minor keys). Remember to write the second chromatic scale directly under the first, note for note, in order to transpose correctly. Try transposing the previous progression into the key of D major.

THE CAPO

The capo is a device which is placed across the neck of the guitar (acting as a moveable nut). It has 2 uses:

1. To enable the use of easier chord shapes, without changing the key of a song.
2. To change the key of a song is a key which is within your singing range, but involves playing difficult chords (e.g. in the key of E♭), a capo may be used.

Capos some in various shapes and sizes.

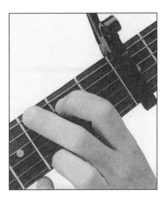

The capo allows you to play the song in the same key, yet at the same time use easier (open) chords. Consider a turnaround in E♭:

If you place the capo on the third fret, the following chords can be played without changing the song's key.

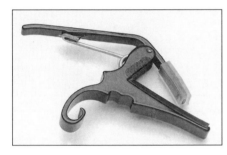

(C chord shape with capo)

(Am chord shape with capo)

(F chord shape with capo)

(G chord shape with capo)

If you have studied bar chords (Section Two), you will notice that the capo is acting as a bar.

To work out which fret the capo must be placed on, simply count the number of semitones between the 'capo' key you have selected to change to* (e.g. C, as used in the above example) and the original key (i.e. E♭ as above). Hence C to E = 3 semitones, and therefore the capo must be placed on the third fret. Expanding upon point 2, consider a song in the key of C, using the turnaround progression:

A singer may decide that this key is unsuitable for his or her voice range and may wish to use the key of, say, E♭. The progression, transposed to E♭, will become:

Instead of changing to these new chord shapes (i.e having to use bar chords), the guitarist may still play the C, Am, F and G chords, but must place the capo at the 3rd fret to do so.

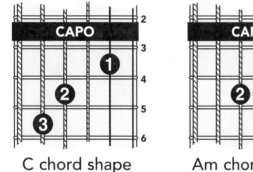
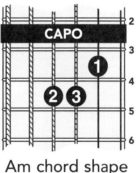
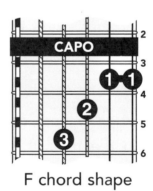
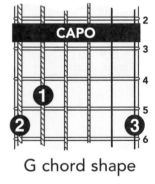

C chord shape   Am chord shape   F chord shape   G chord shape

Original key:

New key:

* Remember you are not actually changing key but merely the chord shapes, for ease of playing.

APPENDIX FOUR - GROUPS

A successful group is not just a mixture of good musicians. You will need to be aware of the many other factors involved in order to avoid the pitfalls that cause many groups to disband within a very short time. The following ideas should increase your awareness of the problems facing a group, and how to avoid them.

1. **Group Direction**

   Before forming a group, you should talk with prospective musicians about their aims for the group. You may decide to form what is called a '60/40' group; the type that plays at cabarets, dances and hotels. This type of group plays a selection of old pop standards (approximately 60%) and 'Top 40' tunes (40%). 60/40 groups can be assured of a steady income, although recognition will not go beyond the local playing scene.

   A different aim for the group may be to play mainly original material in the eventual hope of cutting a record and going on tours. Groups of this type generally do not make much money until they have become well known.

   If you are forming a new group you may find it beneficial to play a 60/40 style to gain experience and money to invest in top quality equipment.

   Decide on the number of musicians, the type of instruments and the basic style of music before forming the group.

2. **Music Choice**

   The style of music you play must be one that is enjoyed by all group members (note just a majority vote). Listen to other bands playing their various different styles and take particular note of the audience reaction in order to gauge the appeal of each style. Once you have decided on a style, aim specifically towards the section of people who enjoy that type of music. This will immediately decrease the number of possible venues for you to play at; but remember that you cannot please everyone and you should therefore aim to play to the type of people whom you will please.

3. **The Group Structure**

   A group can be divided into 2 basic sections; a 'rhythm section' and a 'lead section'. The instruments of the rhythm section include drums, bass (which lay down the basic beat), and rhythm guitar (which 'fills-out' the basic beat). These instruments must co-ordinate to provide the background rhythm; the 'tightness of the group will depend on it.

   The lead section usually consists of lead guitar, vocals and keyboards (which may be used as either a lead of rhythm instrument). The lead instrument acts as a separate voice from the vocals and 'leads' in and out of each section or verse of a song (i.e. an introduction or a 'lead break').

   All instruments must work as a team, in order to provide a combined group sound.

4. **Rehearsals**

   In a serious group you will spend more time rehearsing than doing anything else, so it is important to be properly organised. As far as possible, each session should have an objective which you should strive to achieve.

   Remember that the performance of a song involves not only the music, but also sound balance and stage presentation. These facets should be practiced as part of the rehearsal.

   As well as group rehearsal, you should practice individually. Concentrate particularly on the harder sections of your songs, so that it will be easier to play them when working with the group. It is far more beneficial and time saving for each member to attend group practice with full knowledge of his part.

The underlying theme of all the above topics is one of group unity, both on and off the stage. This is essential if the group is to survive together as an effective musical unit.

APPENDIX FIVE - MINOR KEYS

In music there are two main types of scales, namely majors and minors. The major scale is based on the following pattern of tones and semitones:

		T	T	S	T	T	T	S		
C major	C	D	E	F	G	A	B	C	T - tone
	I	II	III	IV	V	VI	VII	VIII	S - semitone

The minor scale is based upon a different pattern of tones and semitones, as outlined in the A minor scale below:

		T	T	S	T	T	T$\frac{1}{2}$	S	
A minor*	A	B	C	D	E	F	G#	A
	I	II	III	IV	V	VI	VII	VIII

In minor scale there is a distance of one and a half semitones between the 6th and 7th notes (e.g. in the A minor scale above, F to G).

If you compare the C major and A minor scale, it can be seen that they both contain the same notes, except for the seventh note of the minor scale, which has been sharpened. Because these two scales are so similar, they are called 'relative' scales i.e. A minor is the relative minor scale of C major and vice versa. The same principle is applied to chords; the Am chord is the relative minor of the C chord.

Every major scale has a relative minor, which is based upon the 6th note of the major scale; e.g.:

		T	T	S	T	T	T	S
G major:	G	A	B	C	D	E	F#	G
	I	II	III	IV	V	VI	VII	VIII

The E minor scale (the relative minor of G major) will contain the same notes as the G major scale, except for the 7th note (called the leading note) which is sharpened.

		T	S	T	T	S	T	S
E minor:	E	F#	G	A	B	C	D#	E
	I	II	III	IV	V	VI	VII	VIII

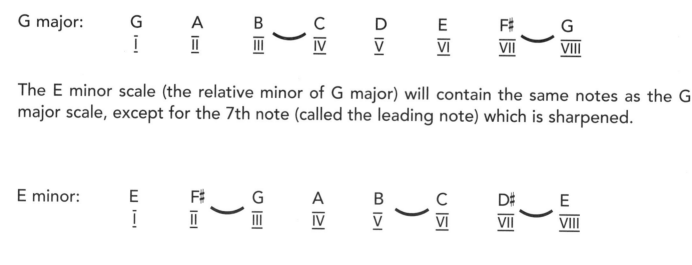

* This minor scale is referred to as the harmonic minor. There are two other types of minor scales, namely the natural (or pure) minor and the melodic minor. These are discussed in more detail in Progressive Lead Guitar.

The following table summarizes the relationship between major and minor keys.

MAJOR KEY	C	D♭	D	E♭	E	F	F♯	G	A♭	A	B♭	B
RELATIVE MINOR KEY	Am	B♭m	Bm	Cm	C♯m	Dm	D♯m	Em	Fm	F♯m	Gm	G♯m

Both the major key and its relative minor share the same key signature, as illustrated in the example below:

C MAJOR
or
A MINOR

G MAJOR
or
E MINOR

D MAJOR
or
B MINOR

A MAJOR
or
F♯ MINOR

E MAJOR
or
C♯ MINOR

F MAJOR
or
D MINOR

B♭ MAJOR
or
G MINOR

E♭ MAJOR
or
C MINOR

The sharpened 7th note that occurs in the relative minor key is never included as part of the key signature. Because each major and relative minor share the same key signature, you will need to know how to distinguish between the two keys. For example if given a piece with the key signature of F♯ thus:

it could indicate the key of G major, or its relative, E minor. The most accurate way of determining the key is to look through the melody for the sharpened 7th note of the E minor scale (D sharp). The presence of this note will indicate the minor key. If the 7th note is present, but not sharpened, then the key is more likely to be the relative major (i.e. D natural notes would suggest the key of G major).

Another method is to look at the first and last chords of the progression. These chords usually (but not always) indicate the key of the piece. If the piece starts and/or finishes with Em chords then the key is more likely to be E minor.

CHORD FORMULA CHART

The following chart gives a comprehensive list of chord formulas, together with an example based on the **C Scale**:

CHORD NAME	CHORD FORMULA	EXAMPLE	
Major	1 3 5	C:	C E G
Suspended	1 4 5	Csus:	C F G
Major add Ninth	1 3 5 9	Cadd9:	C E G D
Minor	1 ♭3 5	Cm:	C E♭ G
Augmented	1 3 ♯5	Caug:	C E G♯
Major Sixth	1 3 5 6	C6:	C E G A
Major Sixth add Ninth	1 3 5 6 9	C6/9:	C E G A D
Minor Sixth	1 ♭3 5 6	Cm6:	C E♭ G A
Minor Sixth add Ninth	1 ♭3 5 6 9	Cm6/9:	C E♭ G A D
Seventh	1 3 5 ♭7	C7:	C E G B♭
Seventh Suspended	1 4 5 ♭7	C7sus:	C F G B♭
Minor Seventh	1 ♭3 5 ♭7	Cm7:	C E♭ G B♭
Diminished Seventh	1 ♭3 ♭5 ♭♭7	Cdim:	C E♭ G♭ B♭♭ (A)
Major Seventh	1 3 5 7	Cmaj7:	C E G B
Minor Major Seventh	1 ♭3 5 7	Cm(maj7):	C E♭ G B
Ninth	1 3 5 ♭7 9	C9:	C E G B♭ D
Minor Ninth	1 ♭3 5 ♭7 9	Cm9:	C E♭ G B♭ D
Major Ninth	1 3 5 7 9	Cmaj9:	C E G B D
Eleventh	1 3* 5 ♭7 9 11	C11:	C E* G B♭ D F
Minor Eleventh	1 ♭3 5 ♭7 9 11	Cm11:	C E♭ G B♭ D F
Thirteenth	1 3 5 ♭7 9 11* 13	C13:	C E G B♭ D F* A
Minor Thirteenth	1 ♭3 5 ♭7 9 11* 13	Cm13:	C E♭ G B♭ D F* A

*indicates that a note is optional.
A **double flat** ♭♭, lowers the note's pitch by **one tone**.
A **double sharp** ✕, raises the note's pitch by **one tone**.

The above chart lists chord formulas for all the different chord types learned and a few additional ones. This is how it works:

B7 is based on the dom7 formula ($\bar{I}$ - $\overline{III}$ - $\bar{V}$ - ♭$\overline{VII}$), and the B scale:

$$B \quad C\sharp \quad D\sharp \quad E \quad F\sharp \quad G\sharp \quad A\sharp \quad B$$

Thus: $\quad \bar{I} \quad \overline{III} \quad \bar{V} \quad$ ♭$\overline{VII}$

$$B \quad D\sharp \quad F\sharp \quad A$$

Major scales not studied in this book can be derived by following the interval sequence tone - tone - semitone - tone - tone - tone - semitone. (See Lesson 26).

ALTERED CHORDS

Other chords that you will occasionally see in sheet music involve a slight alteration to one of the given formulas. The alteration is usually indicated in the name given to the chord. Consider the following examples:

C7:   C   E   G♭   B   **C7♭5:**   C   E♭   G♭   B

The C7♭5 chord is just as the name implies; a C7 chord with the fifth note flattened.

G9:   G   B   D   F   A
G7♯9:   G   B   D   F   A♯

The G7♯9 chord involves sharpening the 9th note of the G9 chord. Another type of alteration occurs when chord symbols are written thus:

Example 1: G/F♯ bass. This indicates that a G chord is played, but using as F♯ note in the bass.

Example 2: C/G bass. This indicates a C chord with a G bass note. Sometimes the word 'bass' will not be written (i.e. the symbol will be just G/F♯), but the same meaning is implied.

SCALE TONE CHORD

In any given key certain chords are more common than others. For example, in the key of C the chords, C, F and G are usually present, and quite often the chords Am, Dm and Em occur. The reason for this is that each key has its own set of chords, which are constructed from notes of its own major scale. These chords are referred to as 'scale tone' chords. Consider the C major scale:

Chords are constructed by combining notes which are a third apart. For example, consider the formula for a major chord:

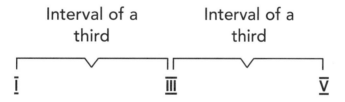

Using the C major scale written above, scale tone chords can be constructed by placing 2 third intervals above each note. This is illustrated in the following table:

$\overline{V}$	G	A	B	C	D	E	F	G	} Third interval
$\overline{III}$	E	F	G	A	B	C	D	E	} Third interval
C Scale:	C	D	E	F	G	A	B	C	
Chord constructed:	C	Dm	Em	F	G	Am	B°	C	

Notice that the chords are named according to their root note (and hence use the root note's scale). However, they are all C scale tone chords because they contain only notes of the C scale (i.e. no sharps or flats).

The method used for constructing scale tone chords in the key of C may be applied to any major scale. The result will always produce the following scale tone chords:

Scale note:	$\underline{\mathrm{I}}$	II	$\underline{\mathrm{III}}$	$\underline{\mathrm{IV}}$	$\underline{\mathrm{V}}$	$\underline{\mathrm{VI}}$	$\underline{\mathrm{VII}}$	$\underline{\mathrm{VIII}}$
Chord constructed:	major	minor	minor	major	major	minor	diminished	major

Thus in the key of G major, the scale tone chords will be:

G   Am   Bm   C   D   Em   F#°   G

and in the key of E♭ major, the scale tone chords will be:

E♭   Fm   Gm   A♭   B♭   Cm   D°   E♭

SCALE TONE CHORD EXTENSIONS

The scale tone chords studied so far involve the placement of two notes (separated by an interval of a third) above a root note. This method of building scale tone chords can be extended by adding another note, illustrated in the following table:

$\underline{\mathrm{VII}}$	B	C	D	E	F	G	A	B	} Third interval
$\underline{\mathrm{V}}$	G	A	B	C	D	E	F	G	} Third interval
$\underline{\mathrm{III}}$	E	F	G	A	B	C	D	E	} Third interval
C Scale:	C	D	E	F	G	A	B	C	
Chord constructed:	Cmaj7	Dm7	Em7	Fmaj7	G7	Am7	Bø7*	Cmaj7	

From this example, the scale tone chords for any key will be:

$\underline{\mathrm{I}}$	II	$\underline{\mathrm{III}}$	$\underline{\mathrm{IV}}$	$\underline{\mathrm{V}}$	$\underline{\mathrm{VI}}$	$\underline{\mathrm{VII}}$	$\underline{\mathrm{VIII}}$
maj7	m7	m7	maj7	dom7	m7	ø7	maj7

*This is the symbol for a half-diminished chord (ø)

G half diminished

(Root 6)

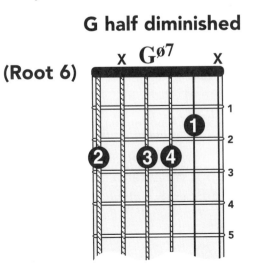

x G°7 x

B half diminished

(Root 5)

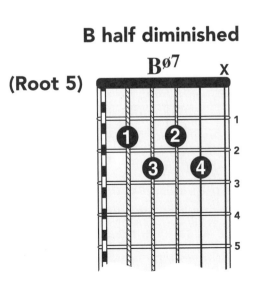

Bø7 x

GLOSSARY OF MUSICAL TERMS

Accidental — a sign used to show a temporary change in pitch of a note (i.e. sharp ♯, flat ♭, double sharp 𝄪, double flat ♭♭, or natural ♮). The sharps or flats in a key signature are not regarded as accidentals.

Ad lib — to be played at the performer's own discretion.

Allegretto — moderately fast.

Allegro — fast and lively.

Anacrusis — a note or notes occurring before the first bar of music (also called 'lead-in' notes).

Andante — an easy walking pace.

Arpeggio — the playing of a chord in single note fashion.

Bar — a division of music occurring between two bar lines (also called a 'measure').

Bar chord — a chord played with one finger lying across all six strings.

Bar line — a vertical line drawn across the staff which divides the music into equal sections called bars.

Bass — the lower regions of pitch in general. On keyboard, the notes to the left of the keyboard.

Capo — a device placed across the neck of a guitar to allow a key change without alteration of the chord shapes.

Chord — a combination of three or more different notes played together.

Chord progression — a series of chords played as a musical unit (e.g. as in a song).

Chromatic scale — a scale ascending and descending in semitones.

e.g. **C** chromatic scale:

ascending: C C♯ D D♯ E F F♯ G G♯ A A♯ B C

descending: C B B♭ A A♭ G G♭ F E E♭ D D♭ C

Clef — a sign placed at the beginning of each staff of music which fixes the location of a particular note on the staff, and hence the location of all other notes, e.g.

Treble Staff ← G Note   Bass Staff ← F Note

Coda — an ending section of music, signified by the sign ⊕ .

Common time — and indication of ⁴⁄₄ time — four quarter note beats per bar (also indicated by 𝄴)

D.C al fine — a repeat from the sign (indicated thus 𝄋) to the word 'fine

Duration — the time value of each note.

Dynamics — the varying degrees of softness (indicated by the term 'piano') and loudness (indicated by the term 'forte') in music.

Eighth note — a note with the value of half a beat in 4/4 time, indicated thus ♪ (also called a quaver).

The eighth note rest — indicating half a beat of silence is written: ♍

Enharmonic — describes the difference in notation, but not in pitch, of two notes: e.g.

F♯ or G♭

Fermata — a sign, ⌢ , used to indicate that a note or chord is held to the player's own discretion (also called a 'pause sign').

First and second endings — signs used where two different endings occur. On the first time through ending one is played (indicated by the bracket ⌐1⎺⎺⎺); then the progression is repeated and ending two is played (indicated ⌐2⎺⎺⎺).

Flat — a sign, (♭)used to lower the pitch of a note by one semitone.

Forte — loud. Indicated by the sign 𝑓 .

Half note — a note with the value of two beats in 4/4 time, indicated thus: 𝅗𝅥 (also called a minim). The half note rest, indicating two beats of silence, is written: ▬ on the third staff line.

Harmonics — a chime like sound created by lightly touching a vibrating string at certain points along the fret board.

Harmony — the simultaneous sounding of two or more different notes.

Improvise — to perform spontaneously; i.e. not from memory or from a written copy.

Interval — the distance between any two notes of different pitches.

Key — describes the notes used in a composition in regards to the major or minor scale from which they are taken; e.g. a piece 'in the key of C major' describes the melody, chords, etc., as predominantly consisting of the notes, **C, D, E, F, G, A,** and **B** — i.e. from the **C** scale.

Key signature — a sign, placed at the beginning of each stave of music, directly after the clef, to indicate the key of a piece. The sign consists of a certain number of sharps or flats, which represent the sharps or flats found in the scale of the piece's key. e.g.

indicates a scale with **F♯** and **C♯** , which is **D** major; **D E F♯ G A B C♯ D.**
Therefore the key is **D** major.

Lead-In — same as anacrusis (also called a pick-up).

Leger lines — small horizontal lines upon which notes are written when their pitch is either above or below the range of the staff, e.g.

Legato — smoothly, well connected.
Lyric — words that accompany a melody.

Major scale — a series of eight notes in alphabetical order based on the interval sequence tone - tone - semitone - tone - tone - tone - semitone, giving the familiar sound **do re mi fa so la ti do**.

Melody — a succession of notes of varying pitch and duration, and having a recognizable musical shape.

Metronome — a device which indicates the number of beats per minute, and which can be adjusted in accordance to the desired tempo.

e.g. **MM** (Maelzel Metronome) ♩ = 60 — indicates 60 quarter note beats per minute.

Moderato — at a moderate pace.

Natural — a sign (♮)used to cancel our the effect of a sharp or flat. The word is also used to describe the notes **A**, **B**, **C**, **D**, **E**, **F** and **G**; e.g. 'the natural notes'.

Notation — the written representation of music, by means of symbols (music on a staff), letters (as in chord and note names) and diagrams (as in chord illustrations.)

Note — a single sound with a given pitch and duration.

Octave — the distance between any given note with a set frequency, and another note with exactly double that frequency. Both notes will have the same letter name;

Open chord — a chord that contains at least one open string.

Pitch — the sound produced by a note, determined by the frequency of the string vibrations. The pitch relates to a note being referred to as 'high' or 'low'.

Plectrum — a small object (often of a triangular shape)made of plastic which is used to pick or strum the strings of a guitar.

Position — a term used to describe the location of the left hand on the fret board. The left hand position is determined by the fret location of the first finger, e.g.
The 1st position refers to the 1st to 4th frets. The 3rd position refers to the 3rd to 6th frets and so on.

Quarter note — a note with the value of one beat in $\frac{4}{4}$ time, indicated thus ♩ (also called a crotchet).
The quarter note rest, indicating one beat of silence, is written: 𝄽 .

Repeat signs — in music, used to indicate a repeat of a section of music, by means of two dots placed before a double bar line:

In chord progressions, a repeat sign ✗ , indicates and exact repeat of the previous bar.

Rhythm — the note after which a chord or scale is named (also called 'key note').

Riff — a pattern of notes that is repeated throughout a progression (song).

Root note — the note after which a chord or scale is named.

Scale Tone Chords — chords which are constructed from notes within a given scale.

Semitone — the smallest interval used in conventional music. On guitar, it is a distance of one fret.

Sharp — a sign (♯) used to raise the pitch of a note by one semitone.

Simple time — occurs when the beat falls on an undotted note, which is thus divisible by two.

Sixteenth note — a note with the value of a quarter of a beat in $\frac{4}{4}$ time, indicated as such ♬ (also called a semiquaver).
The sixteenth note rest, indicating a quarter of a beat of silence, is written: 𝄿

Slide — a technique which involves a finger moving along the string to its new note. The finger maintains pressure on the string, so that a continuous sound is produced.

Slur — sounding a note by using only the left hand fingers. (An ascending slur is also called a 'hammer on'; a descending slur is also called a 'pull off.')

Staccato — to play short and detached. Indicated by a dot placed above the note: ♪

Staff — five parallel lines together with four spaces, upon which music is written.

Syncopation — the placing of an accent on a normally unaccented beat. e.g.:

$\frac{4}{4}$ 1 >2 3 >4 $\frac{3}{4}$ 1 + >2 + 3 >+

Tablature — a system of writing music which represents the position of the player's fingers (not the pitch of the notes, but their position on the guitar). A chord diagram is a type of tablature. Notes can also be written using tablature thus:

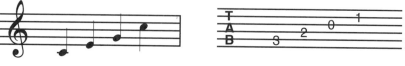

Music Notation   **Tablature**

Tempo — the speed of a piece.

Tie — a curved line joining two or more notes of the same pitch, where the second note(s) is not played, but its time value is added to that of the first note.

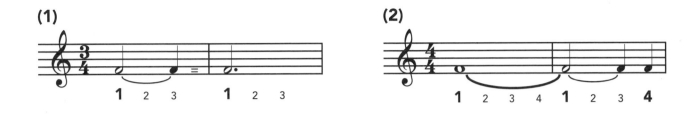

Timbre — a quality which distinguishes a note produced on one instrument from the same note produced on any other instrument (also called 'tone colour'). A given note on the guitar will sound different (and therefore distinguishable) from the same pitched note on piano, violin, flute etc. There is usually also a difference in timbre from one guitar to another.

Time signature — a sign at the beginning of a piece which indicates, by means of figures, the number of beats per bar (top figure), and the type of note receiving one beat (bottom figure).

Tone — a distance of two frets; i.e. the equivalent of two semitones.

Transposition — the process of changing music from one key to another.

Treble — the upper regions of pitch in general.

Treble clef — a sign placed at the beginning of the staff to fix the pitch of the notes placed on it. The treble clef (also called 'G clef') is placed so that the second line indicates as G note:

← G line

Tremolo (pick motion) — a technique involving rapid pick movement on a given note.

Triplet — a group of three notes played in the same time as two notes of the same kind.

Vibrato — a technique which involves pushing a string up and down, like a rapid series of short bends.

Wedge mark — indicates pick direction; e.g: **V** = down pick, **∧** = up pick

Whole note — a note with the value of four beats in $\frac{4}{4}$ time, indicated thus **o** (also called a semibreve).

OTHER BASS BOOKS IN THE PROGRESSIVE SERIES

Now that you have completed Progressive Rhythm Guitar you will be able to continue your music studies with the following Progressive titles.

PROGRESSIVE GUITAR METHOD LEAD

Covers scales and patterns over the entire fretboard so that you can improvise against major, minor, and Blues progressions in any key. Learn the licks and techniques used by all lead guitarists such as hammer-ons, slides, bending, vibrato, pick tremolo, double notes, slurring and right hand tapping.

PROGRESSIVE BLUES GUITAR

Covers all the essential rhythms used in Blues and R&B along with turnarounds, intros and endings, and gaining control of 12 and 8 bar Blues forms. Explains and demonstrates the Blues scale, major and minor pentatonic scales and 7th arpeggios in a logical system for playing over the entire fretboard. Contains classic Blues sounds such as note bending, slides, and vibrato demonstrated in over 100 licks and solos in a variety of Blues styles.

PROGRESSIVE ROCK GUITAR LICKS

This book may be used by itself or as a useful supplement to *Progressive Rock Guitar Technique*. The licks throughout the book are examples of how the most popular lead guitar patterns can be used in all positions on the fretboard, and how various techniques can be applied to each pattern. Several Rock guitar solos are included to fully show how the licks and techniques studied throughout the book can be used to create a solo.

PROGRESSIVE JAZZ GUITAR

A lesson by lesson introduction to the most commonly used moveable chord shapes and progressions used by all Jazz Guitarists. The explaination of chord construction and how they fit into certain keys and patterns will take the mystery out of playing Jazz Guitar. Also includes Jazz Blues progressions, turnarounds and scale tone chords.

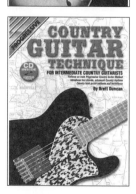

PROGRESSIVE COUNTRY GUITAR TECHNIQUE

This book continues on from *Progressive Country Guitar Method*. More basic chords are covered such as Major Sixth, Minor Seventh, Major Seventh, Augmented and Diminished. This book introduces triplet rhythms, rhythm rests and staccato strumming. The most common Bar chords are also studied and several Country lead guitar patterns and techniques are featured.

Visit our Website: www.learntoplaymusic.com